## A God's Breakfast

FRANK KUPPNER was born in Glasgow in 1951 and has lived there ever since. He has published six books of poetry with Carcanet. The first, *A Bad Day for the Sung Dynasty*, was awarded a Scottish Arts Council Book award in 1984. A novelist as well as a poet, he received the McVitie's Prize for his fiction in 1995. He is currently Writing Fellow at the Universities of Glasgow and Strathclyde.

T0148701

Also by Frank Kuppner from Carcanet

*A Bad Day for the Sung Dynasty*
*Everything is Strange*
*The Intelligent Observation of Naked Women*
*Ridiculous! Absurd! Disgusting!*
*Second Best Moments in Chinese History*
*What? Again? Selected Poems*

# FRANK KUPPNER

*A God's Breakfast*

CARCANET

62

# by the Dogge!

*Acknowledgements*

Some of the poems in *What Else Is There?* first appeared in *PN Review*, *The Times Literary Supplement*, *Poetry Scotland* and *The Drouth*.

First published in Great Britain in 2004 by
Carcanet Press Limited
Alliance House
Cross Street
Manchester M2 7AQ

A CIP catalogue record for this book is available from the British Library
ISBN 1 85754 744 6

The publisher acknowledges financial assistance from Arts Council England

Typeset in Garamond by XL Publishing Services, Tiverton
Printed and bound in England by SRP Ltd, Exeter

# Contents

*The Uninvited Guest*

1

Arise! Already the baker is selling the youths their breakfasts.
And the crested birds of daybreak cry out on every side.


2

The sage congratulates himself for keeping awake
At the very moment when he falls asleep.


3

Perhaps we'll look out one morning and see two sunrises.
I shall not be greatly worried, for I love the dawn.


4

After twenty-five years, he saw the daylight again;
And he looked at it and thought, I do not like this.


5

We are all sleeping figures, dreaming that we are asleep.
Pray God we never wake up, and discover that we are dead.


6

When I learned that Dexter had truly come back from the dead,
I thought to myself, then the case is clearly hopeless.


7

Hearing someone climb the stairway delicately towards him
Faustus thought it might be a Goddess. But it wasn't.


8

We all believe we are special exceptions to the Universe;
No matter how often we solemnly tell ourselves we aren't.

9

I feel I was not given sufficient warning.
Perhaps none of us were given sufficient warning.


10

Modestus at last sat down and wrote the first line of his epic.
But, alas, a bust of Homer then toppled over onto his head.


11

Odd to think that all these old works were actually written.
That someone was always sitting down and writing each one of them.


12

Modestus has written the substance of a truly astonishing book.
But, alas, he has put all the words in entirely the wrong order.


13

There is something so charming about the first lines of epics!
And, for that matter, about the final lines too.


14

Diogenes used to enter theatres just as the crowds were leaving.
Let there now be no doubt that this was a truly wise man.


15

On the day after the public recital, Dama's Great Hall
Again looks so calm, so wise, so thoughtful, so invigorating.


16

'Let nothing evil enter here,' says the sign above Britto's door.
Presumably he himself can get in through a side-window.

17

The finest part of Fronto's new house is the entrance stairway.
Which, all things considered, is doubtless appropriate enough.

18

More than anything else, what I would like to do more of
Is lie about in the morning, in drifts between waking and sleep.

19

Whatever happened to you was whatever was meant to happen;
And if the opposite happened, then that too was just as meant.

20

Something moves by itself. What are you going to call it?
Whatever you call it, it is something which moves by itself.

21

Everything changes into something else.
Except the entire universe. Perhaps.
*[My favourite of them all, I often think.]*

22

Some think the universe is only the universe.
But, fortunately, others have rather less limited views.

23

The Gods made the universe, then forgot all about it.
Every so often it nags at their mind for a fleeting moment.

24

The imagined design of the universe is more harmonious than the real one.
Not that there really is a real one, in actual fact. Terrible line.

25

The First Cause is too important to exist.
How would it let mere reality sully it?

26

In the beginning there was the Void
And it found itself inadequate. *[One knows the feeling.]*

27

We issue from whatever everything else issued from.
There are no two differing ways into the universe.

27b

Oh, no doubt every —— is different from every other, Myson;
Nonetheless we all enter the world in much the same way.

28

That which is real tells us what kind of world this is.
A universe in which real beings dream of another universe.

29

Anything which is real is part of this real universe.
To disintegrate in this one is not to enter another.

30

Dying is not in itself necessarily a sign of failure.
If the cosmos cannot die, then so much the worse for the cosmos.

31

Delius sits in his study, surrounded by busts of his ancestors.
I'm not surprised he is much struck by the expressions on their faces.

32

If I thought every day was a new start, I would kill myself.
I would do so over and over again for as long as might prove necessary.


33

I am in no hurry for posthumous glory.
Or, if it comes to that, for posthumous oblivion.


34

Since Theopompos told me his heirs will publish his poems
I wish all the more that his work was already available to us.


35

At long last, after years of work, Marsus gave his thoughts to the public.
But the public continued to walk past the bookshop nonetheless.


36

Happening to be passing a bookseller's shop,
I continued to go past the bookseller's shop.


37

After the poet's death there was discovered with much pain
A book of brief epitaphs for most of his dear friends.


38

A couple of centuries after the writer's death,
People began to realise he had been much given to sarcasm.


39

From this reclusive library one can still look down on the life of the city.
Which is what so many of the works it contains so greatly seem to like doing.

40

One certainly gets a strong sense of Martial from his poems.
He comes across as a deeply, deeply, *deeply* unlikeable man.

41

One writes couplets, I suppose, from a love of brevity.
But of what use is a long book full of brevity?

42

Some good stuff; more indifferent stuff; much rubbish.
How else is any book going to catch reality?

43

The worst possible reason for writing anything
Is that one is a writer and must write something.

44

Year after year the amount of writing grows.
Will no-one have the courage to stand up and shout 'Stop!'?

45

Thank you for your kind offer, Aunt, of Augustine's *Collected Letters*.
Unfortunately, I have to leave on foot for Caledonia at once.

46

Thank you, Stella, for asking me to give my opinion of your new work.
It was rubbish. But I hope our friendship can nonetheless remain unimpaired.

47

I find myself wondering who could have scribbled 'Utter crap!'
At the end of this beautiful, clean epic manuscript.

48

Who last night chalked on a stairway near the Forum:
*Tantum religio potuit suadere malorum?*

49

It is pleasant to think of Almighty God writing a book.
With what exquisite care he must choose his resounding words!

50

The first rule, Melior, when expounding ageing religious scripture:
Things do not need to mean what they all too transparently *do* mean.

51

God is real, but not as we use the word 'real'.
Or, for that matter, as we use the word 'God'.

52

God may perhaps be best thought of as a sort of light.
Though it is not, of course, much like what we mean by light.

53

God is always something else. Always something else.
The Universe itself is always something else.

54

If a plain bowl can be spoiled by added art,
How much more, Aktor, may a plain universe be spoiled.

55

The first man climbed down to earth on a golden chain from Heaven.
Followed soon after, it seems, by the first priest.

56

The Temple of Jove destroyed by a bolt of his own lightning?
Hmm. Perhaps he has strong views on modern architecture?


57

Every day a new shrine goes up somewhere or other.
At times one or other even falls into disuse.


58

Look at those idiots with their crude belief in the sacred banana.
How unlike us, with our much purer belief in the sacred grape.


59

This God takes a special interest in this group.
And that God takes a special interest in that group.


60

We cannot see thee, Lord, because thou art everywhere.
Almost exactly, in fact, as if thou wert nowhere.


61

I sometimes think that forgetting to exist
Is one of the Good Lord's most endearing oversights.


62

Even after our deaths, Livia, when I have ceased to exist,
And you have ceased to exist, I shall think of you without end.


63

I am not the only one who died too young, I know.
But, somehow, in my case it seemed particularly unfair.

64

I thought our love was greater than the sky itself.
But a tiny, ignorant brute ended it all with a few small bites.


65

The wasp easily discovers how to fly into the room,
But can never find its way out. Is this not love too?


66

It is dawn. And I must leave thy bed, Aurelia.
Or, rather, to be more precise, your bedside cupboard.


67

The passageway from the men's rooms to the women's rooms.
How calm it looks, with a level sunlight lying on it.


68

Even when right beside you, I can't look at you enough.
There is something inadequate about human sight as such.


69

Forgetfulness is annointed in the bedroom.
Few here are not gladdened by the way women can shimmer. [?]


70

Evening. So many lamps are lit all over the city.
And the shadows in so many of them are never your shadow.


71

For hundreds of years, this fish has been called by the same name.
You really ought not to kick it about the kitchen like that, Penelope.

72

The man washed up on the beach had such a wise face.
One would have sworn that he, if anyone, would have survived.

73

What is surprising is not so much that Gabba fell overboard,
As that he cleared the ship's side by quite so great a distance.

74

Yet again Theo celebrated the New Year by jumping into the canal.
But alas, this time for some reason he failed to re-emerge.

75

Gabba thought he would jump off a cliff for the truth.
But, half way down, he changed his mind, and went back up.

75

Some creatures, if cut in two, will become two creatures.
But most creatures, if cut in two, will not.

77

The sheared-off limb falls to the ground in the stadium.
Then, blushing, it sneaks away into the crowd.
[?]

78

Chrestus, having lost both his testicles in battle for the state,
Claimed compensation, and now owns a small, bright, two-room attic.

79

Arriving back from the war, Felicius found much of his house in ruins.
But the front door was still standing, so he opened it and went through.

80

Phoenix was seriously injured when a burning roof fell in,
Hundreds of miles away from the cold lane where he now limps.


81

Melior won a large villa with one lucky throw of the dice.
Alas, his neighbour's mastiff later attacked and killed him.


82

Here lies our dear friend, Bias, who, very probably,
Was the greatest one-legged philosopher that Greece ever produced.


83

While someone was proving to Diogenes that motion was unreal,
He merely sighed, stood up, and walked stolidly away.


84

Aristo has a very rare collection of ancient manuscripts.
He collects only pages where some writing suddenly breaks off.


85

Six hundred people came to Bombus's evening lectures;
And each week one or two went home and killed themselves.


86

For day after day I followed him, enchanted by his eloquence.
How much I wish I could remember a single word he said.


87

Receiving a question in a language it did not understand,
The Oracle nonetheless gave out an answer much the same as usual.

88

If Diogenes had said that, how much it would have been worth.
But alas, Sextus, it was only you who said it.

89

Simon is teaching contempt for wealth again this year;
In a course of twenty talks, at very reasonable prices.

90

Where are all these rich, gullible old women one keeps hearing about?
Am I walking ignorantly past their fine houses every day?

91

The new lad wakes up bright and refreshed, eager for further living,
Though three people have died in that same bed in the last few months.

92

Life and death are both desirable in turn, said Tranquillus.
The misfortune is to die while we still over-value life.

93

Some things, it seems, escaped me. Others did not.
I suppose that was a real life I had, like any other.

94

If I weren't myself, I would like to be Bias of Cyrene.
Assuming that Bias of Cyrene himself wouldn't mind, of course.

95

If everyone had more or less everything he wanted, said Heraclitus,
Things would be more or less the same as they are now.

96

I am happy to be who I am. Which is no doubt just as well,
Since the range of choice offered here is by nature extremely limited.

97

Sweating, Polus entered in mitigation the plea
That he was Polus – and was met with appropriate leniency.

98

Different things may be called by the same name.
Thus, both Polus and I may be called human beings.

99

Plango denies all of his minor crimes;
But, stupidly, fails to deny that he is Plango.

100

Whenever I am in court, listening to some new trickery,
It astonishes me that these people could ever die.

101  *Epitaph*

'Here lies a student of Law who killed himself.
Such self-knowledge is surely rare in one so young.'

102

Everywhere I go, I am worshipped as a God.
Or I would be, if they knew who I really was.

103

I concede it, Crassus. You terrify me.
And if I were someone else, you would terrify him too.
[And if I were two people, you would terrify them too.]

104

We live in an endless cosmos, and are afraid of the dark.
What can happen to you? At worst, it can only get dark.

105

'What can happen you you?', my dear Lucilius,
And 'What can happen to us?', are two very different questions.

106

Zeno held there was no real difference between a short life and a long one.
I wonder, Caesar, if the same might not hold true for penises?

107

A little side-street grove with a statue of a philosopher
And two or three drunks lying on the ground, groaning.

108

Dear God, if ever I am lying on a bed of pain,
Let me be visited by anyone rather than Seneca.

109

One could have no possible remaining argument
With Lucius, if only he would kill himself.

110

When Seneca was ordered by Nero to kill himself,
His young wife too tried to commit suicide. But, surprisingly, she failed.

111

Live as if each day were your last? No. That is morbid.
Live, rather, as if each day were the day after your last.

112

Live each day as if it were someone else's last.
Or, possibly, the second-last of the person just beside him.


113

For years Phyllis made a good living as a hired mourner at funerals.
If she didn't know who the corpse was, she was *incomparable*.


114

Here lies the centenarian Fuscus, who never had a day's illness in his life.
Unless you count the day when he died, I suppose.


115

Once a man feels, 'Yes, I have lived a full life,'
Every further morning is a bonus. Or perhaps completely superfluous.


116

'If you have lived for a full day, you have seen all there is.'
Fair enough. But if you have lived for more than one full day, what then?


117

You have never let us down thus far, Sextilianus;
And we are confident your next failure will be even more impressive.


118

And who invented the tale of Sisyphus, do you think?
Some great mind to whom nothing very extraordinary had happened?


119

How strange this ancient poem on papyrus looks,
Scored out all the way through, presumably by the author.

120

Diogenes, when asked for his view of the universe, once replied:
'A dazzlingly brilliant parody of a lost original.'


121

The universe is a vulture, said Suadeus.
We hardly know what he meant, and yet, we easily agree with him.


122

The universe is a whisper in the dark.
We hear the voice, but we cannot make out the words.


123

It is hard for me to put my feelings for you into words, Caesar.
But, perhaps fortunately, I am still able to fart.


124

Oh ye who prostrate yourselves before God with your arses in the air –
How well do you understand that God is also behind you!


125

Why do the priests behave effeminately in this ceremony?
Why, that is simple, Sextus. Because they are effeminate.


126

How glad I am that I went along to that funeral after all!
I've never seen quite so much pubic hair before in my life.


127

What a *peculiar* object to carve on a tomb, Priscus!
Still: I suppose there must be a reason for it.


128

In life he fought with brambles and weeds everywhere.
And now the brambles and weeds grow over his tomb.


A GOD'S BREAKFAST

129

All I want is to live on for ever and ever
In a non-physical form. Is that so absurd, Postumus?


130

They say that the dead at least need no longer fear death.
But some people are surely stupid enough for anything.


131

After my death, I shall be slowly devoured
By insects of which I know not even the name.


132

The house of Smerdies the doctor is swarming with flies.
So what? One should only be happy they're not souls.


133

Perhaps the soul is air in an extremely subtle state.
So subtle, in fact, that it is no longer air as such.


134

All those speeches which have blown out like a dying gale!
All those unseen kisses which came to nothing!


135

It is not clear whether this beautiful, rediscovered old portrait
Is supposed to represent a Goddess or a woman.


136

First, they take the world to be a sort of statue, which it isn't.
Then they take the statue to be a real person – which it isn't twice over.

137

I approve that Victory here shows only one of her breasts.
To show the full pair of them would amount to a sort of gloating.


138

Peter brings home yet another large, fake statue.
And round it, cooing admiringly, stand his large, fake friends.


139

The universe is surely something like an unwanted gift.
But at least there are flowers growing up between some of the cracks, I suppose.


140

Life is not in itself necessarily a sign of success.
The insects rush around all over the surface of the planet.


141

How much space there is around us, and how much time.
How many small alert animals listening beneath the floorboards.


142

As a few million potential wisps of nothingness, Fronto,
It ill becomes you to take the world too seriously.


143

The wisps combine and couple into yourself.
By all means complain about it while you can.


144

Do not submit to Fate. Make Fate submit to you.
For whatever you manage to turn it to is itself Fate.

145

Strangely enough, no-one is to blame for the entire universe
Nor is the entire universe itself to blame.

146

The dead are now merely a concept in the mind of the living.
Unless perhaps one can still trace some pockets of their dust.

147

We shall be quite unnoticed soon enough, Antonia.
And anyway: who is noticing the whole universe?

148

In the end, there is no such thing as a lasting achievement.
Some take longer to disappear than others do, that's all.

149

There are no posthumous desires, Alexander.
Even the desire for posthumous fame vanishes at death.

150

Better to die happily than unhappily, I suppose.
Not that it makes terribly much difference for long.

151

Most of the great philosophers are dead.
What was it they said about death, do you remember?

152

Here is the tomb of the great orator, Bombus.
What is he saying now, one can't help wondering.

153

Gaius Geminus was easily the wittiest man I have ever known.
Can it *really* be the case that no-one wrote down any of his remarks?


154

The words of this inscription have been worn away.
But since the bust is Caesar's we may be sure they were lies.


155

Why does the treaty run to a thousand words in our language
And only seventy-five in theirs? I just don't trust these people.


156

Textor is a particularly erudite commentator.
He misunderstands his authors in an extremely advanced way.


157

It's all right for the old people in the plays.
At least they had a chorus they could turn to for advice.


158

It is very odd. But since he became stone-deaf,
Critus has taken to visiting the theatre much more often.


159

Critus performed an act of gross indecency
In a public theatre today. Which is to say, he turned up.


160

Titus is a man of taste. He rarely visits the theatre.
And certainly not when his own works are being performed there.

161

You know, the more I think of Oedipus, the more I realise
That Sophocles failed to make full use of its comic potential.


162

In this play, Sleep seems to say rather a lot.
The spectators would like to sleep, but he keeps preventing them.


163

Well, I have seen some cruel things done in my time, Titius.
But to wake up someone who was fast asleep in a theatre!


164   *Epitaph*

This good man woke up, shrieked, and fell dead in a theatre –
Which is something I have often rather hoped for for myself.


165

I have been dead for the whole of my life so far,
And with a bit of luck that's how it will continue right to the end.


166

You shall die and cease to exist. That is all. No need to struggle.
It has happened to so many others already. What does it matter?


167

Of course he is not dead. Nobody is dead.
For to be anything real one must first of all be alive.


168

Life is on the whole surplus to requirements.
A wonderful dream which no-one is quite having.

169

Let us enquire, said the great sage, into whether death is the end.
Let's see now. Oh God, no, it can't be! It can't be! QED.


170

How can we be sure that the Gods have broken their promises?
Perhaps we have merely forgotten what the promises really were?


171

These animals make their own music while they are living,
And they make music for others after they have died.


172

Here lies a brave man who tried to murder a tyrant.
Also in this grave lie five or six of his sons.


173

Theo's parents were more important than mine were.
Why is that, I wonder? It simply doesn't make sense.


174

How often she used to waken up her grandmother
With her shrieks and cries! But now she can do so no longer.


175

Nothing is ever quite as serious as it seems, Lucus.
The complete extinction of the known universe, for instance.


176

The earth will crash, fall to bits, split right in two.
One half will go off that way; the other that way there.

177

Night. The stars seem to run past behind the sky.
In lamplight a man is struggling with a large table. [?]


178

The lamp sometimes throws moving shadows onto the wall.
And sometimes it throws unmoving shadows onto the wall.


179

An everlasting fire, flaring and dying and flaring.
Set by no-one; fed by nothing; consuming nothing.


180

Slowly the strip of sunlight stretches across the room.
And then the neighbouring room. And so on, until sunset.


181

We go to bed and frequently rise again in the morning.
Therefore the stars shall rise and set for ever.


182

For thousands of years huge waves lash against this jagged cliff,
Then, for some reason or other, it suddenly collapses.


183

After about 9,000 lines the epic simply stops.
Either the author just gave up or the copyist lost patience.


184

For thousands of years huge waves lash against this jagged cliff,
Then, for some reason or other, they suddenly stop doing so.
[About 200.]

185

Eventually Sura decided to destroy his old epic,
But still could not quite rid himself of the commendatory verses.


186

Parnasius the scholar loves the epics so much that he has just finished
His fifth book on the subject of *Gross Blunders in Homer.*


187

Rufus always apologises for the fault he has just committed.
Would it not be better, Rufus, simply not to commit it?


188

Rufinus put me up for a day, and I must agree
It was far more comfortable than having to stay in a tree.


189

Spartanus's house has fallen into a grossly dilapidated state.
But frequently his neighbours hear him laughing away in there somewhere.


190

I love to watch the stream swirling through my garden.
Do you, oh my neighbour, also like to watch it as it swirls?


191

In the morning, a dead body was found in the quiet lane.
But, by the evening, it had been removed from the quiet lane.


191a

In the morning, another dead body was found in the lane.
But, by the evening, it had been removed to a much noisier place.


A GOD'S BREAKFAST

192

But for the steps and doors on either side of this lane
I could almost swear that no-one even knows this place exists.

193

Another new house. I begin to grow sick of them.
In which of these buildings will my life be crushed again, I wonder?

194

I seemed to go down a gentle hill for hour after hour.
There was no light. Or just enough light to see by.

195

A spluttering lamp in a window-sill late at night.
If I hadn't come down here for a piss I would never have noticed it.

196

It has long since been forgotten quite why this small suburban temple was built.
Indeed, I dare say that is the main reason why I so often spend some time here.

197

What sort of a lunatic would worship a stone?
No-one. It must be something else they are worshipping.

198

I would quite like to have seen Orpheus play to the beasts,
Provided I could have watched from a suitably safe distance.

199

At length the ship put safely into the harbour;
But all the sailors who manned its hulk were dead.

200

One morning, the ship which had been there outside for weeks
Is suddenly gone. Gone! Gone! Why did I not go with it?

201

A lane of beautiful houses, and I have entered none of them!
In such out-of-the-way places, how they still speak the right language.

202

A dull roar from the distant Circus Maximus.
No doubt someone has won. And someone, no doubt, has lost.

203

Whenever I hear the ready wit of the irrepressible populace,
I find myself looking round for a good place to start a fire.

204

Young Bryson went on a trip to see Babylon,
And returned, astonished at its ruinous condition.

204a

Shrewdly observing my grief at the loss of part of Germany,
Calpurnia sat down in front of me and started gently to play with herself.

204b

Calpurnia has, I think, a particularly beautiful little anus.
I have tried to tell her that, but she can get a little angry.
[Well, from the fact that this one is spelled out in full and the others aren't we
can form a pretty sure opinion of what the dash elsewhere is supposed to stand
for, eh? Oh, yes; I think so.]

204c

The beautiful Virginia's husband is going blind.
I can only suppose he looked at her —— once too often.

A GOD'S BREAKFAST

204d

Why did it take me four, nearly five years to discover
How lovely Julia's —— looks with the dawn sun lighting it up?


204e

I know I hesitated, Julia, when you asked me if your face
Was the loveliest I had ever seen. But I suddenly thought of your arse.
[Here's another.]


204f

Had I known then how strikingly intelligent your buttocks look, Volumnnia,
I would probably never have plucked up the courage to talk to you at all.


204g

There are more unknowns than anyone knows about, Calpurnia,
And more is known and knowable than anybody knows.
[?]


204h

I did not say that literature was for pederasts,
Julia, though I admit I said something rather like it.


204i

Literature is of no importance whatsoever, Manius;
Which is possibly why it can reflect the universe so well.


204j

Manlius is by now mature. Which is to say, he has made
More serious errors than he can keep in mind at any one time.


204k

Manlius is a fat, garrulous, effeminate gasbag, is he not?
How then can his slight daughters laugh so charmingly?

2041

'Thank you for liking so much my tiny, insignificant chest,'
She said once. Oh Julia, you were such wonderful company!

204m

I never feel more keenly that I am not living the life I ought to,
Julia, than when I catch sight of your little ——.

204n

I am a man of principle. I have told no woman that her ——
Was the loveliest in all existence, without meaning it at the time.

204o

I always knew Calpurnia must be an intelligent woman.
But the way she showed off her —— made me surer of that than ever.

204p

When Julia asks me if I wished her arse were smaller,
The only question is, how often should I say no.

204q

When I called her my 'tight barbarian hole',
I suddenly discovered that she was not sleeping after all.

204r

Why do I think they hardly deserve to be women?
Surely I don't still have romantic notions of ——
['Romantic'?]

204s

I suppose I was sorry to hear, Calpurnia, that you were dead.
But I would be sorrier now to learn that the news was mistaken.

204t

The wise man is a citizen of the world,
Since, fortunately, —— is much the same everywhere.

205

How wonderful that women in all countries should have ——.
It almost restores one's faith in human nature. Though not quite, I suppose.

206

I suppose one has to accept that the —— is sacred;
Even though there are some truly dreadful —— around.

207

Plato and Pythagoras were both born of virgins.
After which that trick fell out of fashion for a good while.

208

Some people claim that Moses was a pederast;
But I am fairly certain that he merely didn't exist.

209

Some care deeply about pigs; some about beans.
Truly the religious spirit is almost inexhaustible.

210

How much I admire Plato and his sophisticated view
That our real happiness may exist outside of this real world.

211

Too many things would have to be not illusory
For us to deduce that the whole world is illusory.

212

Philosophy can rid us of many common mistakes,
And perhaps provide in their place a few uncommon ones.

213

This bizarre notion that the body is something else!
That the whole world is in fact something else!

214

Would we call the subtlest music 'non-musical'?
Yet the subtlest parts of the material world are called immaterial.

215

Even to liberate one's will from the material world
Is to act in accordance with the material world.

216

We have ceased to believe that the air itself can think.
Yes. Now we attribute thought to even less than the air.

217

The truly free man, Sextus, does his best to refuse
To be subject to the limitations of mere reality.

218

The encouragement of the delusion that the self does not exist
Is, according to some, the most worthwhile pursuit in life.

219

Oh, millions have fallen in love with real bodies,
But the person they thought existed was almost never there.

220

'I wish three naked women would ask *me* to choose between them,'
Said Parelis. 'Or two of them. Yes. Or even one.'


221

So difficult to sympathise with two people at once.
So much easier to sympathise with the whole cosmos.


222

The universe is not a practical proposition.
Something, it is clear, has badly run away with itself.


223

The world worked out how to fit as it went along.
If it hadn't done so, there would be no world fit to be questioned.


224

We know there is nothing out there beyond the Atlantic, Sextus,
Let fable populate that space however it will.


225

Gently the dawn vapour lifts up off the stream.
Everything is more or less exactly what it might seem.


226

The sun is trying to dry out our garden today, Daphne.
Except that it isn't actually trying to do anything.


227

If Neptune is the sea, we have only the sea.
If not, what is there there more than the sea?

228

Different skies flowing in differing directions,
With all the stars crying out to each other, 'Wait!'

229

I heard a whisper from a calm part of the sky,
Which said: 'Hey, you! You personally will never die.'

230

Any life, however dreadful, has come from a chain of successes in life.
A chain which goes right back to the very beginnings of life.

231

If you could alter Fate, Cleo, it wouldn't be Fate.
Not that, as a matter of fact, there is any such thing as Fate.

232

The retired elderly sage who plants his own food
Is crudely interfering with the work of Nature.

233

'I hear there has been a huge earthquake in Sicily,'
Said Leontius. 'I was there last year myself.'

234

Expiating a vow, Lampo went on a lengthy trip
To the Temple of Fortune, where he tripped and fell over a wall.

235

You are now slightly taller than the statue of Aphrodite
Which has been standing out there in the garden for years.

236

Ferox and his wife like to read Ovid's love poetry to each other.
Or so she once told me when we were sitting together in the garden.

237

Morning and evening, the dignified old lady was carried into church;
Then she came back home and had dignified sex with a favoured slave.

238

One can usually tell when people become truly devout.
They get extremely nervous about who they have their meals with.

239

Meal after meal they consume, surrounded by silent slaves!
Will no-one ever give the signal for the insurrection?

240

Apart from some roars in the Amphitheatre down there,
And a slave sobbing, this afternoon has been a quiet one.

241

The soul is to the body as the scabbard is to the sword.
Except, of course, that one never quite gets to see the sword.

242

'Soul' is a word, Sextus, which stems from the early ignorance
Of how subtle and complex the physical organism can be.

243

I like the view, Didymus, that each of us has two souls.
Though, needless to say, I prefer the view that we have three of them.

243a

Thomas believes we have a soul. He is a very spiritual person.
His brother believes we have two souls. He is an even more spiritual person.


244

When Tertia turns her head so that her face is visible
At the same time as her buttocks, I thank the Gods for my third eye.


245

On Sardo was washed ashore a decayed corpse with two heads.
Did it merely fall overboard? One somehow doubts it.


246

Why do you repine, Gripo, at having only one eye?
After all there is only one sun in the one universe, is there not?


247

Which of us has never seen a face in the clouds?
Or, for that matter, never seen a face *as* a cloud?
[Tears?]


248

A morning shower suddenly makes the street difficult.
Are we really not still sleeping? Neither of us?


249

For a long time, Pastor clung to a rock in the sea.
Then he was swept off and more or less disappeared at once.


250

I thought at first it was Apollo I saw in a dream.
But I now realise it was something else entirely.

251

The corpse of the sailor was at last washed ashore in Malta,
And now lies in an island which he never saw during his life.


252

Ah, if our footsteps were indeed to heap up behind us, Irene,
What a different landslide we should all be threatened by!


253

Quintus likes being in the way. That is his hobby.
Sometimes he will travel great distances, merely to be in the way.


254

I do not object, Quintus, that you force your way into my house.
But it seems to me you might at least not criticise the free food.


255

Life is a dinner party without a host.
And, frequently, without a dinner party either.


256

Heat, scents, voices, seep through most of our walls.
Sometimes all at once. Sometimes only a voice.


257

The air flows through one house and then another.
Yet there was always air in that other house too.


258

All I want from history now is a quiet clean bed.
And not too much noise from the neighbours, if that is achievable.

259

My neighbour likes to gag his wife and then worship her backside for hours.
But I find it works almost equally well without the gag.

260

Fundanus's wife has such an adorable bottom,
I have listened for hours to his absurd views on politics.

261

Married to a self-centred argumentative pederast –
Small wonder that Socrates' wife was a famous scold.

262

Maturus has lately become completely impotent.
And yet, his wife does not look to me like a dissatisfied woman.

263

Due to marry Secundus, Placidia instead killed herself.
One presumes she had not yet seen his penis, but who knows?

264

Dexter divorced an actress, with tears in his eyes.
Much as he had once married her with tears in his eyes.

265

When I was told how many lovers Mephiticus had had,
I wept to consider how stupid so many women could be.

266

One must take so much on trust in order to write a book
Claiming that there is nothing we may confidently rely on.

267

The mice have started to eat the books in my new villa.
They gain more sustenance from Aristotle than I ever did myself.

268

Given that he has completely ceased to exist,
Epicurus must surely be very happy by now.

269

Some things change for the better, Marcus. Some things change for the worse.
And some things change, apparently, for the mere sake of change.

270

If we do not know what it is that causes these things, Marcus,
How can we know that they are caused merely by chance?

271

All our history, Gaius, is a local accident.
But that would be equally true of any alternative history.

272

What do we care what other lives our atoms may once have been part of?
Nothing like that lives on. We are only who we are.

273

Having ceased to exist, one has ceased to do anything.
Actually, one is no longer even crumbling away.

274

The dead are merely a concept in the minds of the living.
Once the minds that hold them go, they are entirely gone.

275

How many of us have been put to death carefully?
Many more have breathed their last, unseen, in quiet rooms.

276

Do you ask me, Sextus, what happens to the flame of the candle
Once it goes out? That is simple. It ceases to exist.

277

The more picturesque the past appears to us,
The more egregiously we have failed to understand it.

278

One goes up the stairway in one attitude, Iris.
One comes down the stairway in another attitude.

279

How many roots had to be chewed to bring us here?
How many braids of hair had to be plaited together?

280

They say this village was overrun by snakes and abandoned.
I am almost frightened by how greatly I feel at home here.

281

Piso was a large man, but a statue of his genius,
Rendered life-size, could be knocked over by a small worm.

282

If Publius had been healthy he would never have written his epic.
A profound argument, my friend, for proper diet and exercise.

283

Celsus has worked in a cold-storage house for so long
That he must surely find the *Aeneid* almost congenial.

284

Virgil wrote the *Aeneid* because he felt he had to.
Almost the worst possible reason for writing anything.

285

In one respect at least Philip greatly resembles Odysseus.
He likes to be tied up not far from a naked female singer.

286

Here lies Spurius the grammarian, whose main pleasure late in life
Lay in listening to foreign women chewing his irregular verbs.

287

Sacerdos has reached that age when he cares for nothing but food.
Ideally served by young sailors who are, effectively, nude.

288

How do I solve the celebrated paradoxes of Zeno?
Simple. By pointing out that the man was a pederast.

289

The Sceptics too try to defend their views by good arguments,
But where their arguments are bad their position defends itself.

290

Anything may be anything else at all,
Provided one's manner of speaking be loose enough.

291

To concede the merits of an objection, Honestus,
However forthrightly, is not quite the same as to answer it.

292

Oh, Heraclitus! Oh, great mind! Oh, great man!
Of all philosophers the most worthy to misunderstand!

293

No. It is not quite that he solved the great religious problems.
Rather, that he failed to do so in such uniquely brilliant language.

294

Honestus is such a forceful advocate of truth-telling
That once he even told a demi-Goddess to stop lying.

295

His faith was far too pure to be troubled by such questions
As whether or not he had answers to its mere technical difficulties.

296

The preferred solution, Sextus, to many deep conceptual difficulties
Is often the mere inurement to the fact that they exist.

297

Aphlatos insists that such and such just must must be the case.
Then he looks around hopefully for signs of helpful arguments.

298

God told me to do this. God told me to do that.
Which is to say, I decided to do this and that.

299

And were the Gods themselves perhaps chosen by an election?
Did they put up proposals, perhaps, and get themselves voted in?

300

The Omnipotent has at last vanquished his enemy!
What a triumph! Eh? Who would have expected it?

301

Alas, the great old stories are being forgotten.
And, what's worse, the terrible new ones are being made up.

302

Modestus the prophet used to receive in his dreams messages from God,
Which he would sell on to others for a very modest profit indeed.

303

Vaticanus asked the Oracle if perhaps he was at risk
Of being blackmailed. And now he is being blackmailed.

304

It is very easy to make an accurate oracular production.
Simply make it after the event and date it to before.

305

Mind arranged everything, before anything was there.
Before even mind was there, I suppose. Why not?

306

By misunderstanding a verb, he seemed to do the impossible.
And when it was understood, too many people believed in him.

307

Chrestianus the philosopher greatly admires the truth.
Rather as one might admire the crests of distant mountains.


308

All this verbal pursuit of virtue, Socrates!
Just try to be virtuous in the rough sense of the term.


309

Plato was on bad terms with everybody.
Even Socrates called him a liar, did he not?


310

Plato I think castigated Anaxagoras
For being too concerned with the merely real world.


311

The easiest way, my friend, to put one's rivals to flight
Is to invent stories in which they are put to flight.


312

The Goddess of Poetry has been particularly active
Where Troilus is concerned. His work has entirely vanished.


313

The wrath of the Gods is slow. Which is to say,
If you wait for long enough, bad will befall anyone.


314

Everyone, Sextus, has unrealistic views about everything.
The astonishing thing is that anyone is right about anything at all.

315

It is futile to wish that life were something else entirely.
You can move only the pieces on the board as it is.

316

Liars applauding liars, all knowing they are liars.
And no-one saying that word. And thus it continues.

317

We find we are in a race, but do not know over what distance.
Is that the finishing line over there? No. No, it never is.

318

He who lives through each day as if it were his last
Will be a calm bore who is mistaken all but once.

319

In his later years, Fuscus completely forgot his name and identity.
Thus his life may be said to have ended up as a marked success.

320

Are nine years and ninety years really the same in eternity, Marcus?
Which of them would you have preferred your child to live for?

321

You know, the previous Emperor but three was a very good man.
I often saw him, sitting in a large chair, wincing stoically.

322

From the Stoics one is left with a distinct impression
That the truly wise man would have seen to it he had never been born at all.

323

Have you lost your son and heir, Caesar? But why weep?
There must be at least fifty philosophers you could refer to in this connection.

324

This king apparently could speak five languages like a native.
One wonders what he cried out as his sons hacked him to death.

325

I hate my father for not drowning me at birth.
But perhaps he felt much the same about his own father.

326

The same Greek word can mean a marriage alliance or sorrow.
Some call this a double meaning and some do not.

327

Few women ever forgive you for not loving them.
And fewer still, Turnus, forgive you for loving them.

328

Each of us was once carried about in a bag
Whether or not our cases are now stuffed full of inaccurate biographies.

329

Pontifex's translation of Homer was virtually flawless –
Except that he sometimes confused the Trojans and the Greeks.

330

If Issa the philologist has a single drawback, it can only be
That often he appears not to know what the words mean.

331

Do not dare to say 'Good morning' to Socrates,
Unless you have time for his million words of answer.


332

The classic punishment for the relentless bore, I seem to recall,
Was to be tied into a sack with the complete works of Livy.


333

If poor spelling is indeed a sign of genius,
Then Thallus is perhaps a rival author to Homer.


334

Plato never mentions Democritus, but not for reasons of envy.
Nothing like that, no. He never mentions Xenophon either.


335

Apparently none of Poemander's plays survive.
He is by far my favourite tragedian.


336

Glenis is so old he has forgotten who he himself is.
Which is surely the wisdom of age, if ever I heard it.


337   *Epitaph*
When I was young I was young; and when I was old I was old.
And one seemed by and large to be much the same as the other.


338

Years ago I was forced to choose between tooth decay and impotence,
And I am delighted to say, my son, that I chose a dignified impotence.

339

For years I feared I had lost you. Then for years
I feared I might have to keep you. Oh, the unending fears!

340

Poet after waiting poet seems never to have realised:
The girl did not turn up because she was far too frightened to.

340b

This is hardly surprising now is it, Didymus?
Would you choose to meet a poet if you didn't have to?

341

Many things which terrified during the night, in the morning
Are revealed to be objects of laughter. And the opposite too, alas.

342

The worst thing about serious illness, whispered Faustus,
Is that so few people get to see how incredibly brave one can be.

343

Who would have thought a field could retain so much blood?
Or is there perhaps some other explanation for this charming effect?

344

Tomorrow dust and moisture will be what you are,
And occasional words between two or three people, at most.

345

All these fatal diseases! I wish I knew which one
Will carry me off, Hippocrates, so I could respect it more.

346

What's that lying up at the top of the stairway? A corpse?
No. Nothing. It is merely a shadow and a vat. All right?


347

Never give a box to anyone with the instruction
Not to open it. These things are against nature.


348

Yes, yes, Gaia – I did indeed say I would die for you;
But that was before you brought me a rope for a present.


349

Something was floating in the lake for many hours.
We thought it might be a body, but eventually it sank.


350

Not all reforms, my darling, are necessarily for the best.
The old form of human sacrifice was surely much better than this.


351

One doesn't really believe in any of these ancient armies.
Their weapons, we think, could not really draw blood from these bodies here.


352

Observing his child's brains scattered all over the front hallway,
Archie the philosopher thought profoundly about Pythagoras.
[What?]


353

The mere fact that these people are called perfect
Is itself argument enough not to run after them.

354

Leo the Philosopher is an extremely arrogant man.
Which is just as well, as I cannot counter his arguments.


355

Let us sing the praises of the unintelligible!
After all, it is hard to see what else we can do with it.


356

The universe has farted immensely in all our faces;
And we try to ignore the huge stink as best we can.


357

While Sulpicia bounces her noble old boobs in my face,
I sigh at the thought of the chances I have lost in life.


358

One lesson I have learnt, Sextus, from my travels to innumerable places.
It is vitally important not to fart in important people's faces.


359

Ariston the Bald, I think, considered the whole universe
To be a sort of fine wig on an imaginary head.


360

Though Celtus died in a foreign war, extremely far from home,
Friends brought back one of his toes and buried it in his garden.
[Not one of his eyes, darling?]


361

When what makes us what we are no longer exists,
Oh, how we shall exult in our perfect freedom!

362

So many great tribes have died out, and yet Polus still exists.
What filthy bribe can his ancestors have given to the Gods?

363

Perfect freedom means freedom from everything.
Freedom from mere existence, to give but one example.

364

Unable to show that the Gods exist, Paulus
Contents himself with saying it is certain that they exist.

365

At best, this man assumes what he ought to be proving.
Though frequently, indeed, he cannot manage even that.

366

Paulus seems to think, the absurder his beliefs,
The more respect his beliefs deserve from others.

367

Arrius has much to say about other people's lack of humility.
And what is his tone of voice? Humble? No; I don't think so.

368

No, Marcus. I cannot believe that the ultimate in wisdom
Consists in behaving as if the world did not in fact exist.

369

When the universe is at its worst it continues to exist anyway.
Whether advantage or drawback, it continues anyway.

370

The universe is an unclaimed, illegitimate child.
Fortunately, Spurius, I was elsewhere at the time.

371

Everything is always changing, and we throw words after it.
A few of them stick; mostly in the wrong place.

372

The will was born in chains, yet everywhere is now free;
Chiefly because the chains have become so unfollowably elongated.

373

I wonder sometimes if the whole world might not be a fraud or a fake.
But the dog follows me trustingly along the path anyway. *Suade!*

374

Another chariot passes over the crest of the hill,
Then begins to speed down towards the country.

375

A dog labours over the crest of the hill,
Then begins to speed up back towards the city.

376

A little boy walked past me in the street
With scratches all over him. Hmm. Zeus, I suppose.

377

Pyrrhus was struck dead by lightning as he sat in a boat.
But then, he wasn't *really sure* he was on a boat, was he?

378

Did I fall asleep for a moment? I rather suspect I did.
There is something strangely altered about all those shadows.

379

Is that ship down there going in another direction?
Or is it slower than us? Or is it not moving at all?

380

How can you say the moon is as large as it seems to be?
Are all those distant ships as large as they seem to be?

381

So Hippasus the Mathematician was drowned at sea, was he?
If only the same had happened to Mathematics itself!

382

The world is a sort of round stain on a table, Demetrius.
Is it water, or something rarer? Who can quite say?

383

Reed beds run along either side of the river.
Many are writing in this continent. Many are writing in that.

384

Though he wrote, among much else, several dozen biographies,
Almost nothing whatsoever is known of Plutarch's life.

385

Why are there so many insufferable shits in Athens?
Why, because, I suppose, there are so many people in Athens.

386

These flies live only for a day, which, quite frankly,
Seems enough to me. In fact, rather more than enough.

387

Flies do not seem to have much sense of shame.
All in all, they fit into Athens extremely well.

388

Atoms and the void only – unless perhaps the void
Is merely no more than a subtler sort of atom.

389

The entire universe is a wild scatter of mud.
But what a wilder net of light at times shines through it!
[Can a net shine?]

390

Few things are easier, Marcus, than to show that God exists.
Simply pick some good thing which exists, and attach the word 'God' to it.

391

If I were the constructor of the whole world, Lavinia,
I too, I think, would prophesy with great confidence.

392

If God wants you to do it, you will do it.
And if he doesn't want you to do it, then you won't.

393

God, the great surgeon, binds up the wounds he has given;
And his creatures recover, unless he wishes them not to.

394

God likes to help those who try to help themselves.
As indeed he should, since none can do anything without him.

395

What happens tells us nothing whatsoever about the Gods –
Unless, perhaps, it is something to their advantage.

396

'To be everywhere,' said Seneca, 'is to be nowhere.'
Well worth pointing out to God, if ever one could locate him.

397

Satyrus is stupid enough to be an atheist.
How then does it come about that he is *not* an atheist?

398

How can such a bad man be so profoundly religious?
Perhaps religion helps him reach the depths of his badness?

399

Some priests have raped their charges; some have robbed them;
And I dare say some have done neither. Truly, it takes all sorts.

400

Perennial wisdom established within a church? No, Aulus.
The perennial wisdom is: never to trust a church.

401

They do not believe in the Gods. They hold secret debauches.
They have no faith in the State. We know who these people are.

402

Though the Empress rarely left her bath, she did many good works.
And even the bad works she did were performed very cleanly.

403

Even in a palace one can live chastely and with great dignity.
Or one can run around in the nude shouting, 'Bounce! Bounce!
    Bounce! Bounce! Bounce! Bounce! Bounce! Bounce! Bounce!
    Bounce! Stop it!'
[I think perhaps you have taken this too far.]

404

'Do it now!' she shrieked. 'Do it now!' And I was greatly impressed
By how much of her charm her voice retained nonetheless.

405

There is always a lovely scent of perfume in the perfume shop.
Unless Sodamos is there, buying a present for his girlfriend.

406

I would rather sniff at your bush than at any bush in flower, oh Thais;
Though I admit I have never been much of a botanist.
[Literally, 'a Theophrastos'. Or Theophrastus.]

407

This flower is reputed to be a cure for impotence, Zoilus.
Why not have a hundred of them delivered to your house?

408

This flower is reputed to be a cure for insanity, Troilus.
Why not have a thousand of them delivered to your house?
[I think these two would be better the other way round.]

409

She entered the house and lay down, while I inspected her private parts.
But we soon both realised there had been a very serious misunderstanding
    indeed.

410

I am greatly disappointed in my new husband's erection,
Said the shy, newly-married Prixo. Shouldn't it stick out at the *front?*

411

Mutto's marriage was ruined by his mother-in-law's tongue.
She laughed far too loudly when he mounted her in the vestibule.

412

Livia was happy to let me pretend to strangle her.
But how could she be so sure I was only pretending?

413

'Nowadays I quite like having my failing parts rubbed by old women,'
Said Saturninus. 'Strange, isn't it – how it always has to be women.'

414

There used to be a rather charming little brothel just across the lane there.
Shall we ask that distinguished old gent at the window what he might remember
   of it?

415

My neighbour told me there are nine adulterers in this street.
Which surprised me, as I knew of only seven people who lived here.

416

Your retirement villa, Sabinus, is indeed well hidden down this leafy lane.
But I found some local women who could direct me to it with impressive ease.

417

Xande is such a quiet lover. In fact, this morning
She was so quiet I feared she had left. But she hadn't. Not quite. No.

418

How strange to discover that trembling, bad-tempered Chloe
Also has such a charming, quiet and classical flap at the front of her.


419

I lifted him up from the floor. He groaned and farted.
So I put him down again, gently. This time he merely farted.
[I have changed the gender here, which I suppose, as some requitement for the
ridiculous extent of my exhaustive and unacknowledged labours, I surely have
every right to do.]


420

It was no defeat, Massa, to die like that.
You could not have fallen to your death in a nobler way.


421

Even suicide can become something of a fashion.
But, alas, Gabba has never been very sensitive to mere fashion.


422

Chrestos was condemned to death in the Amphitheatre last night,
Even though he was merely a member of the audience.
[And the odd thing was, he was only tuning up at the time.]


423

Maccius the actor played a reprieved murderer last night –
But, alas, the crowd voted to let the capital judgement stand.


424

Soso was such a dazzling embezzler and manipulator,
It is impossible to believe he could not also somehow cheat death.

425

I dare say I am not as brave as my neighbour Alfius was.
On the other hand, I'm the one now sitting here talking about the battle.

426

What a wonderful story Pontius told us yesterday!
I can't remember any details, but it was quite wonderful.

427

Cicero can remember all his long speeches perfectly.
And I can forget them all equally perfectly.

428

Surely even the most acute aesthete would feel little better
To hear his death sentence read out to him in flawless verse?

429

We are very sorry to put you to death, O Socrates.
But, alas, our own divine sign has commanded us to do so.

430

Since Socrates told the court he would not be joking, Sextus,
They could hardly be blamed for taking his nonsense seriously.

431

Every day, Chrestus looks down from his attic to the statue of Justice,
And congratulates himself on being above the law.

432

Dama's view of being properly dressed differs from most people's.
With him it is a question, first and foremost, of wearing a money-belt.

433

Give me at once whatever spare cash you have, Fuscus,
So that I can embark on my proudly independent life.

434

Formerly Mercury was the patron saint of thieves.
But when the Church came in there was no longer any need of him.

435

After traversing much of the town, the open sewer
Sinks underground just before reaching the Great Saint's house.

436

During the wedding night, the roof fell in
And killed the rejoicing couple. So. No anti-climax for *them*.

437

Not a few are killed by their first heart attack, Leo.
And not a few are killed by their second heart attack.
[On the other hand, no-one is ever killed by both.]

438

When I was twenty, I thought forty would be quite enough.
But now I am thirty-five, I quite like the look of a hundred.

439

By now, Thais, you are ancient, rank and withered,
And of interest only to perverts. Still. The world is full of perverts.

440

Having just eaten a rare fish which came from another world,
Fucinus clambered upstairs and did something else next.
[something even more appalling]

A GOD'S BREAKFAST

441

Poking away at his washerwoman's rugged buttocks, Fucinus
Is shocked by the sudden tenderness he feels for the back of her large head.


442

Those who think Caligula is lacking in human warmth
Having obviously never watched him chat to his wife's backside.


443

Lalage has never been known to say, 'I apologise.'
But fortunately, 'Are these pretty?' seems to work just as well.


444

Fundanus's wife has such a sublime bust,
I have listened for hours to her absurd views on theological matters.


445

Envy is more than a third of politics, Verus.
And poverty is more than another third of it.


446

The problem with a secret ballot, as Pliny pointed out,
Is that no-one can tell how anyone else has voted.


447

Why did they never put a black mark against Nepo's name?
Was it because the name itself was thought to be black enough?


448

I do not consider you to be a pervert, Spurinna.
But then, I do not consider you to be anything.

449

Is Sacerdos famous merely for having a tiny cock?
No, indeed. He also once saved three sailors from drowning in Pannonia.

450

Some of them have little ticks, and some of them have big ticks.
And much the same may be said of the passing moments, I suppose.

451

Serenus has nine or ten houses scattered about the city.
Even when he is at home he is rarely at home.

452

All those people in the villas on the hill
Shrieking in terror at every mild creak they hear!

453

Stella was buried in the gardens of the Temple of Virtue,
Which he so often haunted at night with a few recent acquaintances.

454

I do not know whether it is the best or the worst of his followers
Who were insistent that Heraclitus had a penis made of pure mercury.

455

Epicurus enabled those people to live calm, happy lives
Who would probably have managed it without him anyway.

456

Before turning to philosophy, Chrysippus was a long-distance runner –
An art which many of his listeners later felt a great longing for.

457

In due course Socrates will be remembered
For what he was good at. As a pederast.


458

Macedo's mind is fraudulent, but so highly polished
It affords one great pleasure to watch him slide out through the door.


459

Genitor, who trained for years as a boxer,
Later became expert at knock-down theological arguments.


460

Of course Socrates was not a buffoon.
Or, at the very least, not a very funny buffoon.


461

I once asked Pudens if the wise man ever lost his temper.
But he merely laughed in my face and called me a squinting, stinking
    child-molester.


462

True sagacity means, Gabinia, the profound knowing
That one knows nothing. A rare triumph indeed!


462b

If the profoundest wisdom is to know that one knows nothing,
Then you, Hister, would seem to be very nearly there.


463

If applause and philosophy do not mix, Lucilius,
Then perhaps you are truly a philosopher.

464

Socraticus, explaining why his wished-for beliefs arose,
Seems to assume that he is thereby proving them to be true.

465

Having repeated an objection which he cannot answer,
The Great Saint seems to think he has by now answered it.

466

Everything is chance which cannot be explained.
Once explained wrongly it can rise to become religion.

467

At least half the criminality of history
Results from taking gross fictions for the literal truth.

468

Everything disperses, which is probably just as well.
And even if it isn't, everything disperses.

469

Socrates thought he knew nothing – and I agree with him.
Oh, I'm not entirely serious – but then: neither was he.

470

Nasta and I are very much alike.
He is not afraid of anything, and I am afraid of everything.

470b

So great is our capacity for closing our eyes to the truth,
The amazing thing is that anyone ever gets anything right.

471

The cause of something is some of what went before.
But so often, Marcus, we know nothing of what went before.


472

Thank God I did not live in the Golden Age!
But I dare say I would have tarnished it soon enough by my mere existence.


473

Serenus thinks the world is more or less perfectly good.
His views do not allow him to take much notice of reality.


474

Hair grows on our faces and we start to observe the world.
A gale blows over the wall we were sitting by long ago. [?]


475

Today I shall make the Gods fall off their seats.
Or whatever it is they are sitting on, if not seats.


476

What might the Heaven be like of which this new sage raves?
It sounds like a sort of brothel one can never be thrown out of.


477

Those who assail the Gods as relentless pederasts
Must be very careful where and when they bend over next.


478

What is that which lifteth up the moon in the morning's cool?
The finger of God, is it not? No? Surely not his tool?

479

Clarus says that he has never had a single dream in his entire life.
But I cannot believe that, for I have seen his wife.


480

The universe is more beautiful than one of your labia, Callo;
But perhaps not quite as beautiful as the pair of them.
[This must be breasts.]


481

We know that life is bitter, and yet we produce children.
But our parents too must have made a very similar mistake.


482

If women couldn't dance, argue and take their clothes off,
I am not quite sure what I would have found to do with most of my life.


483

This book which I began when both my parents were alive,
I now end, O Penelope, when my only child is dead.


484

Always we should be able to say to ourselves,
'The universe might end this morning. So what?'
[No; not this morning. Perhaps this afternoon.]


485

'Let no-one see you hurrying,' said the old sage Chilon once.
And my father much liked the sound of this, though he never could quite
   say why.
[My father quite liked the sound of this, and often repeated it.]


A GOD'S BREAKFAST

486

A miracle! Charmus finally won a crown at the races!
Yes. He took third prize in the sprint which followed his own.


487

I walked five miles to see you. But you were not at home.
Or perhaps you were too busy. Anyway, I walked ten pleasant miles.


488

First of all a dummy is flung into the ring
To make the bull angry. This is our life, Theone.


489

Fingers do indeed point you out in every crowd,
But they do not all point you out for the same reason.


490

You are a wonderful person, Clarus. And so is your wife.
Now, kindly give me some money. There. Is that clear enough?


490a

The difference between fighting off imaginary serpents
And fighting off real ones can't be all that great, I suppose.


491

The more I see of money, Titus, the more I have contempt for it.
Oh, how I would like to be able to afford an infinite contempt!


492

A philosopher could not tell you whether Clarus was happy or not.
But I very much suspect a decent banker could.

493

In this book I intend to reveal the hidden intentions
Of the mightiest Gods. Now. What will you give me for it?

494

Trebellius has written an allegory which may be read in three different ways.
But, alas, no-one seems to want to open the thing at all.

495

The poetical pioneer stumbles across a variety of new faults.
His followers then pick out one or two of these and work them to death.

496

I read your book, Flaccus, with great enjoyment, straight through.
Only now, two days later, do I begin to see how bad it was.

497

God cured the great saint of the faults he had built into him,
In order that he might, by this means, have no faults.

498

I was Postumianus, a grammarian. And my conclusion?
That living is merely a tmesis within oblivion.
[?]

499

There are few adoring spouses who remain adoring
After they have read the diaries of their beloveds.

500

As little illness as possible and let me die in my sleep
Is all I ask of you, Gods. Oh – and make my book a success.

501

Accept, Liberia, I beg you, these distichs of Didymus;
Not all of which are distichs or, indeed, go back to Didymus.

502

I shall never see the roofs of my native city again.
But, fortunately, I can see roofs from this window beside me.

503

Fortune, Natalis, rarely enters through the main door.
She comes in through a side window, and exits through a crack in the floor.

504

Phoenix, having escaped with his life from a great fire,
Built a votive church in gratitude – which, alas, soon burned down.

505

So, the Sacred City has been utterly destroyed!
With a bit of luck, that's the last we'll ever hear of *them*.

506

Everyone who disagrees with them is, at best, an idiot.
But they try to be as humble about this as they possibly can.

507

Go back far enough, and everything is exponentially implausible.
Mind you, Sextus, a lot of it is grossly implausible close-up too.

508

'Oh dear me!' cried Skeptos, the enthusiastic disciple of Pyrrho.
'I have just slain my wife. Or, at least, I suspect I have.'

509

I have never known a woman who demanded as little attention
As Leontion does. I wonder if she's quite all right.

510

'That makes at least five black men I have seen today,' said Evadne.
'I wonder where on earth they are hiding all the women.'

511

There is nothing about you that I do not admire.
Certainly not the fact that you do not admire me.

512

That which no longer exists can hardly much care
Whether or how it's remembered by some trick of the universe, can it?

513

Death has such an unfairly poor reputation.
As indeed, for that matter, has public masturbation.

514

Yes, I note the reference here to Diogenes, Lucilius.
But is *private* masturbation very highly reputed? I think not.

515

Zeno called beauty the flower of chastity.
Or did he perhaps call chastity the flower of beauty?

516

Heraclitus is not a complete waste of time.
There are few philosophers of whom one can say quite so much.

517

Oh, loveliest of all sights in an artist's house!
A long, bright, plain surface not yet contaminated!

518

Turnus likes to write his poems on the back of scattered papers;
Which explains why the Muse so often turns her back on him, I suppose.

519

Does the Muse time and again turn her back on you, Sparsus?
Then why not take the hint, and stop sniffing about?
[The ms. says 'start' – but this is obviously a mere mistake.]

520

How odd that with no bust and hardly a great backside
Doris still has enough beauty to keep me fully awake till dawn.
[Because you're just so bloody special, I suppose.]

521

It's not as if I ever begrudged him my arse either,
Shouted the young widow angrily at her mother.
[What complete and total bastards some of these people are.]

522

Despite her flat-chested appearance, Helladia is not a lad.
Every other part of her proclaims this. As, indeed, does her chest.
[Oh yes. So mature! I changed the name, of course, to retain the priceless play on words. It would have been such a tragedy to lose it!]

526

Everyone who walks out of a house is [a] Ulysses.

528

For many years, Leo has not left his own house.
<But then, neither has he left anyone else's.>

529

I rather like not knowing who my new neighbours are.
<Neither in the universe, nor just across this narrow lane.>

533

Perhaps we shall be reborn, completely paralysed.
<Yes. Living for an eternity, completely paralysed.>
[It is hard to know quite what might have happened hereabouts. The metre of the second line here is quite wrong, as if someone had misremembered or had somehow botched an attempt at memorial reconstruction.]

535

She clasped and unclasped her fingers upon her knees.

537

Heavy wagons have been passing this room all day.
[Pretty much the same here too, what with the cars and so forth.]

540

Smoke stains the air for a moment, then disperses.

542

Each day some miner or other is left beneath the earth, dead.

544

To find the universe exciting is to have failed.
<And to find the universe unexciting is also to have failed.>
[Now this, which, though tediously mechanical, is presumably a matched pair from a single source. It does not seem to leave much, if any, room for success.]

545

Everything that is past lies together, nowhere.
<Everything that is future lies together, everywhere.>
*[And perhaps this too, which sounds suspiciously like an exercise. As do a few later ones.]*


547

The old level of the sea rises and falls.
And the new level of the sea rises and falls.


550

Matter tries to arrange itself this way and that way.
Yes. Matter tries to arrange itself that way and this.


551

The old are like that largely because they are baffled.
The young are like that largely because they are baffled.
*[Is this indeed what was meant, or has one line (presumably the ending of the first) somehow corrupted the other? Emendation seems particularly pointless here (Gorgo-Porgoe, for instance, would replace the first 'baffled' with 'tired' – whereas Occcam would replace the second 'baffled', rather temptingly I admit, with 'young'), given that corruption is by no means certain.]*


552

There is no quicker way to do it. One must work.
I touched the mother and ran away down the corridor.
*[By now something has gone pretty radically wrong. This one is clearly two quite separate halves. Perhaps two leftovers inexpertly stitched together?]*


555

Imaginary messages from imaginary beings[.]
*[What is this? A first line shorn of its consequence? I doubt if it should end with a full stop. Just possibly there should be an exclamation mark.]*

556

But it was the fifth wave that did for the ship.
*[And here we must surely have an orphaned or abandoned second line. Not a first line anyway, though time and chance have left it free-standing.]*


557

Lightning strikes at the sea again and again.
*[We are now back to something which sounds like a first line which has somehow been stripped of its mate.]*


558

Suppose, said Plato, we had spent all our life in a cupboard.
*[Or 'coffin' – the word is ambiguous. Alas, this sounds like another start we would have welcomed the continuation of.]*


559

We are all caught up in the prison of actual existence.


560

Democritus has the whole universe back to front.
*[Now, suddenly, an undeniable one-liner. I suspect, in fact, that this is a marginal note by the original anthologist – or by one of them anyway. To the best of my knowledge this is a completely original suggestion. However, I see no reason to question unduly the traditional supposition that what immediately follows, to a considerable extent, is a collection of aphorisms (whether entirely or preponderantly) by Democritus – the so-called, grotesquely misnamed, 'laughing philosopher' – or those of his sect. Many are, technically, in poetic form.]*


561

The Gods created the world, but left it empty.


562

The universe is clearly an act of insanity.
[The universe is clearly an act of revenge.]

563

The universe is an explosion which has nowhere to explode in.

564

The universe is a bad place and we do not wish to leave it.

565

The universe exists because it might as well do so.

566

One impossible joined with another and made the actual.

567

In the end, there is an adequate reason for nothing.
[And are these last three examples really separate? I suspect that Nos. 565/566, 565/567, 567/565 and 567/566 could all be made to work as couplets with very little, if any, reworking.]

568

The universe is an erection which nearly always fails.

569

The other world is a rhetorical effect.

570

Perhaps the entire universe is a slight mispronunciation.
[Oh yes? And how exactly? Perhaps this is part of a riposte to an accusation of speaking bad Greek – the sort of thing which the Greeks seem to have been unusually prone to do.]

571

Surely the entire universe cannot be a disease?

572

I am haunted by the fear that the entire universe is the wrong size.
*[A difficult fragment, perhaps – especially to the linguistically inept. But I for one have not the slightest doubt that the above is exactly what it amounts to. (Heu's view that the writer is saying, in effect: 'I expect the entire universe must be pretty hopeless in bed,' is self-evidently anachronistic and absurd, and no doubt merely reflects personal preoccupations of his own, presumably well-founded. I suppose it may be a joke.)*

*Not, indeed, that I believe the thing really is a fragment either. What we have here, I expect, is a rare one-line epigram. It is, note, a perfect example of the extremely demanding amachicolaic or so-called Thyestean metre – which is not the sort of technical feat which one would wish to maintain for terribly long. Another example, perhaps an even more famous one (see No. 536: 'Once they develop a shape, that's it. They know too much.'), is now generally considered to be spurious – though not, I should perhaps at once add, by me.]*

573

The universe is winning a game which no-one else can even play.

574

So much of the universe is a matter of opinion.

575

To most of us, the universe must be a considerable disappointment.

576

The universe is the result of a failed bet.
*[A joke? Few things can be more tedious at times to the weary than the ancient sense of humour.]*

577

The universe is a sort of loud noise made by cows.
*[Moo, presumably. Or, if* mu, *an unexpected example of cultural overlap!!]*

578

I don't suppose the world could have been hurled from a catapult?
*[Bradley suggests here a philosopher in a comedy indulging in (deliberately?) crude cosmological speculation? Rather like Bradley himself, one might suppose.]*

579

There is much in the air which supports life, and much which supports death.


580

I wonder if the earth is not in fact a disease.
*[Suspiciously like No. 571 above, which Bradley Jr. in fact prints as the second line of a distich, using No. 580 as the first. One can certainly understand why he does so — a fairly rare experience with this editor.]*


581

This would be a good day for the earth to split in two.
*[From a tragedy? There certainly seems to be something vaguely Herculean about it.]*


582

The creation occurred because the Gods like destroying things.


583

The Gods are playing games which are subtler than they are.
[   ]


584

I very much like the thought of God being darkness.
*[But this rather negative thought seems to contradict No. 663, if we are to think of this series as coming from a single source.]*


584b

Even to say 'I know nothing' requires such a world of knowledge.


586

To renounce the world is to fail even as a failure.


587

The truly good do not die, until right at the end of their lives.
*[Might this perhaps be a parody of a some tragic platitude? Of course, it may also merely be such a platitude itself.]*

587a

How strangely impressed so many other people seem to be by their own deaths.

588

Even whirling the sky round and round must ultimately tend to boredom.

589

Our entire history is a weed rotting [?] round a grave.
*[A very obscure word, not to be found in Carterius's supposedly 'complete' Lexikon. It may simply mean 'rustling'. By the singular 'weed' is perhaps meant a single clump of weeds.]*

590

Chance is a name attached to our limitless ignorance.
*['Chance favours the unprepared mind' (Hovelack).]*

591

To no-one belongs the credit of inventing language.
*[Perhaps because, as Organm puts it, silence is better?]*

592

The word 'God' always fits into the metre.
*[A remark of very considerable malicious resonance.]*

593

All sacred texts are, in effect, forms of human blackmail.
*[One would think Democritus must be far too early for such a sentiment.]*

594

We shall know the Gods by the strange smell they give off. [?]

595

I must say, Destiny seems to have no dress-sense at all.
*[Obscure. This appears to be the likeliest meaning – though I admit I don't quite know what the meaning actually amounts to. 'One never quite sees Destiny in the nude,' according to Camus. But then, who would want to?]*

596

Death is not a state which the living ever occupy.
[*And vice-versa.*]

597

We pass on the torch of extinction from one to the other.

597a

I don't much care how I die, provided I don't keep shitting myself.
[Is this not very like one of the ones that went earlier?]

598

Any normal day will feed us, with any normal food.

599

More happiness at one friendly breakfast than in the whole of Homer.
[*Not by any means the conventional view of Homer, certainly.*]

600

It would be a mistake to take Odysseus too seriously.
[*Ditto. Compare No. 161.*]

601

Death has an unfairly terrible reputation.
[*This is virtually the first line of No. 513, given earlier. Who can say why it has been repeated here, if this is indeed the repetition.*]

602

Much that had seemed impossible in the end almost does itself.

602b

After forty-five years, the war took a turn for the worse.
[*Epic parody?*]

603

Everything that is not embarrassing comes from the Gods.

604

The creation of the insects was not a friendly act.
[*Not even for the insects? This seems a bit harsh.*]

605

Everything emerged, connected with everything else.

606

Perhaps one day the sun will just go off somewhere else.
[*This strikes me as being funny, for some unknown reason.*]

607

Perhaps one day the sun will just go off somewhere else again.
[*With Brodlaugh, I presume the repetition is involuntary. Bradley replaces 'sun' with 'moon' –
which at least gives some point to the matter, but is, alas, wholly without any manuscript
justification. Much like the earth itself, I dare say.*]

608

Life is a wonderful dream which no-one is quite having.
[*A fragmentary, perhaps earlier, version of No. 612 below.*]

609

I like to think of the dead as laughing uncontrollably.
[*Or 'that the dead are, etc.'. Perhaps this especially needs a context.*]

610

Heaven is a dead place with a cold wind blowing through it.

611

Nothing is immortal. Certainly, nothing that lives.

A GOD'S BREAKFAST

611a

Nothing is essentially timeless.

611b

Only nothing is essentially timeless. [Or Nothing.]

612

Life is on the whole surplus to requirements.
A wonderful dream which no-one is quite having.
*[An expanded version of the earlier monostich, No. 608b above. Unlikely, one feels, to be from the same author.]*

613

None of us ever got quite what was destined for him.

614

The soul desires nothing, except perhaps to exist.

615

Fortunately I have lived my entire life in another place.

616

History is a vast crowd that we are not part of.

617

Make your next move from where you actually are.

618

No behaviour will make it possible for you to live for ever.

619

If you must practise to be good, then go ahead. Practise!

620

The virtuous life is an affront to Nature.
*[Direct antithesis of the Stoic view. But this must be a joke.]*

621

How *arrogant* all the people who disagree with me are.
*[Another joke, presumably. Just possibly, a self-righteous voice from a play.]*

622

Socrates passed on his views as a direct message from the Gods.
*[Is this supposed to be connected to No. 621, by any chance?]*

622a

Of course, dear Plato is perfectly entitled to his *opinion*.

623

The Whole is a sort of curtain which may not be swept back.
*[A domestic metaphor, rather than one from the drama, I would think.]*

623b

Why would anyone want to have insight into reality?
I would much rather acquire insight into something a bit more interesting.

624

The mind is a sort of mist which is even subtler than mist.
*[This saying is usually attributed to Heraclitus.]*

625

I suppose a man may at least piss into the same river twice?
*[But this, though it obviously refers to Heraclitus, is equally obviously not by the great man. Clemens thinks it may be an excerpt from a comedy, but it is hard to envisage a realistic stage situation of the time where such a remark would be plausible.]*

626

'There is not quite enough emptiness in the cosmos,' said Heraclitus.
*[Not according to any other commentator on Heraclitus, alas. Of course, one feels very reluctant to attribute such a remark, in tone so reminiscent of someone invoking an 'old classic', to someone who was so near to being Heraclitus's contemporary.*

*Gum's suggestion, that perhaps it was another Heraclitus who was being referred to, is self-evidently absurd – as well as being the sort of self-serving evasion of a real difficulty which is pretty well always open to anyone.*

*Evidently, you cannot quote from the same Heraclitus twice.]*


627

A sky which is hostile to us has set itself in motion.
*[Lovehack's brilliant suggestion that some of these utterances are or were meant to be taken as the utterances of an oracle – presumably a real one rather than a fictional one – has in the last three years gained so much scholarly ground as to already be pretty well the general consensus on this vexed matter. I have embraced this supposition in the present work, and tried to take it a little further – though with how much success it is not for me to attempt to estimate.]*


628

Something I do not trust is suspended in this air.
*[A classic example of oracular polysemousness, surely.]*


629

We all of us breathe more air than we really require.
*[A very puzzling remark indeed. I expect it must be corrupt. Mind you, I dare say a good few of the most celebrated philosophical insights here included must be corrupt.]*


630

The earth is full of strange things which would like to kill or eat us.
*[No more than the truth, Verity.]*


631

All our lives we must carry these appalling weights about.
*[Presumably this has something to do with the human conscience. (Dalhousie suggests it might be from a play on a mythological theme. Yes. But which theme?)]*

632

Plato's basic insight was a form of mental illness.

633

There are far too many ships on this sea, I tell you.
*[I doubt very much if these are actual ships.]*

634

Some people spend their whole lives fearing the end of their lives.

635

If we must kill other people, let us at least kill them fairly.
*[Irony?]*

636

Man should take good care that the Gods give him the correct attributes.

637

That which is without joy cannot be the best.

638

In fleeing death, we flee life.
[Because that which creates one has simultaneously created the other?]

639

~~Whenever you see a corpse, try not to laugh.~~
*[A squib directed at the Pythagorean school?]*

640

If everything is everything else, why avoid anything?
[The limitations of existence are existence itself.]

641

The dog sniffs at the milestone, pisses, then hurries on.
*[Perhaps an emblematic if somewhat crude image of terrestrial existence?]*


642

I have noticed that it is only in fables that lions really speak.
*[Might this be a lion speaking here? In a fable? Or is this too far-fetched?*
    *On the other hand, one has to take risks, or one might as well be completely silent.*
    *I realise some would prefer the latter.*
    *'If a lion could talk, a lioness would soon tell it to shut up.' (Alice Floewe).]*


644

No man shall be buried in two places at once.
*[Is this perhaps a parody of a legal or religious decree? In which case it should possibly be placed beside No. 639?*
    *Oldschar gives 'burned in two places at once' – which is presumably a mere misprint, even for him.]*


645

Only a Great God could commit patricide twice.
*[One would love to know the context of this rather dazzling observation. How much I find myself hoping it wasn't merely a joke. I dare say we all do.]*


646

Slowly the passing feet wear the streets and stars away.
*['Stars', despite Stearns, is undoubtedly correct. By no means a routine philosophical observation.]*


647

I suspect that women don't really give birth to children.
*[Perhaps from some such farce as* The Extremely Suspicious Old Man. *An elderly husband is having the wool pulled over his eyes?]*

648

I'm sure that statue wasn't there last week.
*[From a play? Let's try a sheer but well-meaning guess: someone has blundered into the wrong house after coming back home from a drunken debauch and is waking up in the wrong garden? (Good title for an autobiography, by the way!) One somehow feels one has seen this scene several times in the course of one's life, whatever it may more precisely amount to, if anything.]*


649

I would rather keep my private parts throughout eternity, thank you.


650

I shall never forget what she looked like up in that tree
*[Metre and common sense alike suggest that this must be from a farce.]*


651

Suddenly trees leapt forth out of the earth.
*[Corrupt? Or a poem on a mythological subject? Or, of course, quite possibly, both.]*


652

Which of us has never seen a wrong face in the clouds?
*[As in No. 274.]*


653

How delightful it would be, if we could find ——s in eggs.
*[Those who cannot live without filth will no doubt find their curiosity suitably rewarded elsewhere.]*


654

How on earth can women possibly fill up with milk?
*['Fill up' with milk! Presumably some bemused male in a city comedy. 'The shaky grasp of physiology might well be the author's own.' (Perthaps.)]*

655

All that is really required is that one's mother's private parts be able
    to function normally. Given that, the rest follows. One need not
    ever like them; or, certainly, ever see them.
*[A prose fragment. The reason for its being included here is completely opaque. One feels it
could have been jotted down anywhere, for any reason. That it survived at all is, I fear, a minor
tragedy in itself.]*

656

I am very sorry that the old word for '——' has died out.
*[Such does indeed seem to be what it means. See my remarks on No. 643 above. I shall not
dignify this piece of male crudity with the least further discussion. We have had enough of that
by now. More than enough.]*

657

Everything that changes is brief, if you want to call it brief.
*[Or 'if you must call it brief'.]*

658

I have been someone else for the last three years.
*[Usually lazily included among the aphorisms – but surely an excerpt from a play. Maybe
about one of those Greek heroes who dutifully killed his mother? No shortage of candidates
there.]*

659

I would like to have been present at the invention of money.
*[From a play? This is a voice one would gladly have heard more of, whoever it more exactly
might have been.]*

660

Kindly keep such remarks for your next life.
*[Ditto. From a comedy, obviously. I very much suspect an irreverential treatment of the
Alkestis theme, but, needless to say, I can't prove it.]*

661

I suppose I was vaguely hoping to be dead by now.
*[If this really did come from a tragedy, as Theword suggests, then it sounds like it might have been the most charming tragedy ever written.]*


662

We have been falling through the sky for a very long time indeed.
*[From an epic, one brazenly guesses.* Icarus? *(But in that case why 'we'? Or are his broken wings perhaps speaking?)]*


663

Never trust what happens in unnecessary darkness.
[Compare to the other one.]


664

Is the flame worse off after its extinction than it was before it was struck?
*[This is in fact (at least as preserved here) a prose sentence.]*


665

All night long the fire has burned on the distant shore.
*[Distinctly Homeric.]*


666

The thousandth and last ship sails away from the sacked city.
*[A start evidently, but of what? It sounds more like an epic than an epigram.]*


667

The sound which the stars emit is an endless scream of pain.
*['The most horrible remark I know of which was left to us by the ancients,' according to Untergruendemichi (But surely No. 597 is even worse?)]*


668

Well: if it is not part of Nature, what is it part of?


A GOD'S BREAKFAST

669

The universe is a pederast pretending to be a clock.
*[Hmm. Those interested in learning more about how time was measured in classical antiquity should look elsewhere. There are by now many such treatments in existence. If this isn't spurious, then what is?]*


670

At the most unfortunate point, the husband's false teeth fell out.
*[We may, I think, be grateful that the rest of this, whatever it was, is lost. It reads like part of another manuscript entirely. Was someone using the back of it to scribble down jokes on, or what?]*


671

If a man cuts off thy head, then do thou likewise.
*[One feels that this crude and obvious parody of a Biblical injunction can hardly have been a free-standing remark. It is clearly very late, even if not quite phoney. Actually, I suspect it is phoney. None phonier.]*


672

Alas, in a law-case Philip called a spade a spade.
*[This sounds like a genuine one-line epigram to me. The consequences of Philip's appalling forensic solecism were clearly serious, but are better off not being limited by being made too explicit. Thus, all the editors' attempts to supply some putatively 'missing' second line are, in my view, just so much misplaced effort. Quite apart from the fact that, by the way, Socrates of Byzantium, in the fourth or fifth century, seems to say that the majority of these poems have three lines!]*


673

Art is the perfume sprinkled on a privy.
*[A famous trope, of course. Not a very Greek sentiment, I should imagine.]*


674

Suddenly thirteen ladders appeared at the top of the wall.
*[From a Trojan epic? Perhaps the same source holds good for No. 602?]*

675

Strange fate, to produce oneself the very fingers which strangle oneself!
*[Obviously from a tragedy, or from a parody of one at the very least. Of course, in a sense, 'All tragedies are parodic' (J.F. Kupozyk).]*


676

Why did our fathers not speak the same language as we do?
*[A resonant question, indeed. If an aphorism, it can hardly be meant literally. Perhaps from an Aeschylean play about exile?]*


677

So many expressions on the faces gone!


678

On second thoughts, I would quite like to be dead.
*[Wit. Possibly part of a conversation? It can hardly be from a serious play. Distinctly unHomeric.]*


679

There is something strangely heartening about the thought of dead clowns.
*[This is my best understanding of what this self-evidently somewhat technical term must allude to. 'Priests' (Jadinn), can hardly be right. 'Comedians' (Haco, in the modern sense), is just about possible. Where Massed gets 'torturers' from is presumably a private matter for him and his psychiatrist.]*


680

Another flaw of old age is that it does not last long enough.


681

Write briefly, but use as many words as you can.
*[Again, without better knowledge of a context, this must remain highly elusive. I suspect it is something of the nature of a joke, never the easiest of genres for the academic approach to deal with.]*

682

Actual hand movements produced all those texts too.
*[Reminiscent of No. 11, very far above. Ah, how young we were then! Priest suggests a marvelling piece of marginalia by an annotator, which has somehow been assimilated into the text. One is tempted to suggest, in a spirit of vain emulation, that human existence as such is somehow an annotation which was inadvertently assimilated into the text. But the expression could no doubt benefit from a little more work on it. Again, perhaps rather like the universe. But that's enough brilliance for now.]*

683

I hate it when the Oracle uses the word '——'.
*[The hateful word in question has been removed at some time or other long ago, and thus I am spared the stern moral necessity of removing it myself; but I dare say that those who take the reference here to be to the* pudendum muliebre *will, as usual, not be greatly mistaken. God knows, its fecund absence seems to have seeped in almost everywhere here. Is one perhaps supposed to be flattered, or what?]*

684

A trembling woman is hiding behind each tree in this garden!
[I don't know, darling. I despair sometimes. This could be anything.]

685

Lesbia was helping men right from the day of her birth.
*[Reply from an oracle? If not, one would rather not contemplate the content here more closely.]*

686

A billion —— later, are we any happier?
*[If I had the courage of my convictions, I would just cut this piece of nothing out too. But, alas, scholarship has its mindless yet unshakeable conventions, like so much else.]*

688

We struggled along a high path covered in blood.
*[From a tragedy, presumably. Why anyone wanted to gather such shards together remains, despite all our best endeavours to illuminate it, a complete mystery. Certainly, I have never read a convincing overall explanation of the phenomenon. One assumes it was the result of some sort of deliberation.]*

689

I returned, but the entire city seemed to have vanished.

690

Suddenly he understood there was a crowd in the forest.

691

Stranger, do I owe you anything? No? Then kindly get lost.
*[Evidently, a rather disobliging tomb inscription.]*

692

To discover the secret of the universe is to fail badly.

693

Why can we not discover the secret of the universe?
Simple. Because there is no secret of the universe.

694

To call love the secret of the universe is to misunderstand it totally.

695

Do you call love the secret of the universe, Charito?
It would be slightly less inaccurate to give that name to ——.

696

Oh well, the actual universe is at least a start, I suppose.
*[Just possibly from a play, I suppose. Obviously, by now the pickings are getting very much slimmer.]*

697

The Holy Spirit within ourself *is* ourself.
*[This seems to have wandered in from a completely different manuscript tradition. Presumably it is not another of these later Christian interpolations which it is always so easy and convenient for the lazier commentator to discern or invoke.]*

698

I have had much experience in teaching rain to weep.
*[Unless this is merely corrupt, it certainly sounds very oracular.]*


699

How much rain old Rome had to put up with too!


700

'If I must be a moth, let me at least be a moth in Athens.'
*[Is there perhaps, as Demost suggests, some allusion to Socrates here? See next.]*


701

Socrates claims to know nothing, and I for one believe him.
*[The present tense is interesting. But it can hardly be from Democritus.]*


702

Oh, Socrates. Leave the words and look at the real world.


703

If we did not trust each other, we would not have arrived here.
To have got here at all required a fit in things.
*[I'm not sure this isn't two separate monostichs which have at some point been run together.*
*The sentiment behind the first may be cornucopiously generalised, of course.]*


704

I do not want to still be here when the plants start laughing. [?]


705

The wave of a vast ocean clatters unseen in my heart.

706

All that water flowing through the great city!
[*Perhaps also the start of a satire? I cannot help suspecting that Heraclitus might well be due for a mention hereabouts too.*]


707

This trickle of fresh water has saved thousands of lives.
[*One is inclined to give up. What thanks does one ever get for it? This could surely be a part of, or the start of, just about anything. For that matter, it would make a fine ending to something like a topographical* mythos *or lyric.*]


708

Molten wax is running across the floor.
[*Let it run. Why try to stop it?*]


709

My father too sank slowly under the waves.
[*From a mythological poem?*]


710

That over there is perhaps the throat of the universe.


711

Modestus has breath which smells like rotting corpses.
[*Comedy? Just possibly, as Gum suggests, the start of a satirical epigram. But why would anyone wish to preserve the* start *of an epigram?*]


712

How many dead people are running through our dreams?
[*Or, for that matter:*
'*How many dead people are running through our dreams!*'
*The start of one poem, I suppose. But which?*]

713

I'm having terrible trouble forgetting my life completely.
[*I sympathise.*]


714

Blood poured down for hours onto the path beneath.
[*From a tragedy?*]


715

At least our ship was wrecked on a celebrated rock.
[*From a comedy, presumably. For want of any better suggestion, I simply take these to be some of the snippets which took the fancy of the anthologist, perhaps predominantly during his sojourns in the theatre.*]


716

Never mind, father. We can try again at the next palace.
[*Presumably, a parody of a tragedy? Certainly the metre gives countenance to such a suggestion.*]


717

As a consolation prize, please take this small empire.
[*Very obscure. This is the best I can do with it. Bladess, typically, thinks a type of cake is being discussed! It is plainly the pay-off in a comedy.*]


718

Someone is standing outside my house, shouting things.
[Not *'Someone is standing outside my house, shouting "Things!"'*, *whatever stale jokes Occamb might prefer to make on such matters. But I suppose we all have to earn our professional reputations as best we can, each playing to our own particular strengths.*]


719

I heard a whisper from a calm part of the sky.
[*Again, very like something from a tragedy. Someone is obviously losing control.*]

720

A huge cavern opened up before me in the sky.
*[Ditto. And very near to being a continuation of the previous.]*

721

The bars are falling from heaven! I too shall enter!

722

By a sudden miracle, the world was turned into a desert.
*[Late. Perhaps a parody on a Christian theme?]*

723

There was a time once when the inhabitants of Hell were happy.
*[If this truly is the first line of a 'Christianising' poem, as the late Dr Strathgunboyd of blessed non-memory once proclaimed to all and sundry, particularly if they were young, male and good-looking, and perhaps devout, then one could indeed very much wish that more of it had been preserved.]*

724

Whoever heard of a believer killing another believer?

725

Another dull, victorious shout from the remote Circus.

726

I draw the line at my mother-in-law's arse.
*[From some mercifully lost comedy, presumably.]*

[From this point onwards, it may be as well to assume that we are dealing predominantly with spurious and disconnected fragments.]

726

Life is, in the end, a raving absurdity.
Does everyone have to find that out for himself?

726a

Does life seem less ridiculous in the torture chamber?
When one might wish it particularly to end?


726b

To try to describe weeping is not the same as to weep.
To try to understand laughter is not the same as to laugh.


726c

One sees the strength of religion. How helpful to be given reasons,
However specious, for supposing that one matters to the universe as such.


726d

Cocohortus insists that his views involve a profound paradox.
But see them as golden flatulence and the paradox dissolves.


726e

Philosophers think that philosophy is the ultimate enterprise.
Though, as far as I can see, nobody else does so.


726h

One thing we can say about Caesar: he was a man of intense emotions.
Yes indeed. At least he didn't kill thousands of people coldly.


726i

This latest ruler is, alas, not even a pederast.
What he loves about females is their comparative physical weakness.


736k

Forgive me, Hippoturdus, if I described you as an ageing bumboy.
I mistook you for someone else of the same name.

726m

Time is a sort of vapour thrown off by difference.

727

Hail, coinage! The greatest of all human inventions!
[This reads very like another first line. A parodic ode?]

728

Madam, I saw your father's blood drain right out of his head.
[This sounds more like a line from a play. A tragedy, presumably. Or I dare say it might be
from a parody thereof.]

729

How much of it would have been possible without horses?
[Indeed. So much done by climbing up on top of other animals! At such moments it becomes
obvious that the Creator, if any, must indeed have had a quite wonderful, if slightly malicious,
sense of humour.]

730

All real angels are compulsive kleptomaniacs.
[But I wash my hands at this. 'Post multa virtus opera laxari solet,' remarked the Great
Seneca somewhere or other, who can say quite where. Or, as the schoolboy translated it: 'After
opera there is much virtue in a laxative.' How we both laughed! Even the tropical fish seemed
slightly the happier for it.]

731

Let's see now. I have to prepare lunch for one of them
And fascinate the other.

732

Once you have seen *one* set of entrails escaping out of a body

733

That gentleman walking down the lane there is in fact God.

734

The girls pissing in that ditch over there are in fact God.
*[All right. Some see a distich here, with No. 733; but I take the second to be an irritated parody of the first. The whole thing, much like life, has a strangely unconvincing air to it.]*

735

God does not exist, but not in the sense that we mean by 'exist'.

736

God does not exist, but not in the sense that we mean by 'God'.

737

What a collection of shits there must be in any Paradise.

738

I open the work of yet another supposedly advanced mind.
Yes. Here we go again. Death won't be enough to kill us.

739

Life is that state in which matter can watch things going wrong.

740

I have this terrible fear sometimes that the wicked
Are certain to escape all justice in the next world too.

741

Nothing raises us above material existence.
However high we reach, that is still where we are.

742

What deep thoughts? Kindly tell me what they are.

743

The sad truth is that the entire universe happened too late.

744

There is no such thing as a more than material nature.
Or must we give our self-delusions the grandest possible names?

745

Yesterday Uranius the doctor sat down by the statue of Zeus –
Which this morning lies in shattered fragments all over the benches.

746

One of Machon's children is a girl, and the other is a boy, but what of that?
Both are alike being buggered by a charismatic visiting priest.

747

Who is it stands by my bed in the dark, farting?
*[Ah, the great old questions!]*

748

It seems to me that practically nothing has been said.

749

After we cease to exist, all shall be made
Blindingly clear to us by an impossible being.

750

Rejoice! The entire universe is an unvisited tomb.

751

Just as I thought 'Everything is going wonderfully well!'
Those bloody spots appeared at the end of my nose.

752

There is something about a weeping woman's legs

753

There is no stone so heavy that one cannot throw it over some wall.

754

Many are the great truths which I might have imparted, Hadrian,
Had I had more confidence in the capacity of others to understand them.

755

If the brute beasts cannot see beauty, are they any the worse for it?

756

Basilo thinks the Gods created us in order not to forgive us.
They cannot forgive us our gross impudence in merely existing.

757

Death is not sleep, for sleep requires a sleeper.

758

Death is often seen as the final great gatecrasher, Lavinia.
But surely life too was an uninvited guest?

759

Mercator very greatly adored his first wife.
And perhaps even more greatly adored his second wife.
*[Since 'The opposite of life is more life' (?) (Suadster).]*

760

Why should everything be here rather than there?
Or now rather than then? Who can tell me that?

761

Or why should everything be there rather than here,
For that matter? Or then rather than now?

762

Extract the physical from what exists, and there will be nothing left.
*[A definition of materialism? Prose.]*

763

The universe is too horrible to be true.

764

Oh, if only God could have had a good evacuation instead!

765

Give thanks to God for the mere fact that you exist. Or not.

766

The universe is too horrible not to be true.

766a

The universe is too lovely [not] to be true.

767

The simple fact is that the Gods resent human happiness.

768

Truth is truth, wherever one may find it.
But, no doubt fortunately, one is not obliged to look.

A GOD'S BREAKFAST

769

The butterfly is seen as a symbol of the soul, Mys,
Though it is just as physical as a caterpillar or chrysalis.


770

Earth and Hell exist, but Heaven is for God himself.


771

The non-Existent do not look down on anyone.


772

All these people running around asking what reality is!


773

It is our duty to be joyful, whether we want to be or not.


774

The greatest love is to understand that others
Are as large and as real as one seems to be oneself.


775

Nearly all the deepest literary effects are illusions.
Perhaps this is even true of art in general.


776

What is the name of this play that we are acting in,
Marcus? What is the true name of this play?


777

A cynic is one who wanders around depressing the virtuous
By pointing out truths they would prefer not to think about.

778

Cynicism, Sextus, is the subtlest form of generosity.

779

Yes, yes, yes. Of course you'll live on after you've ceased to exist.
The whole universe couldn't possibly even *think* of continuing without you.

780

If God could imagine God, it would not be anything like a God.

781

I very much object to how ordinary such people look.

782

What sort of bloody stupid name is that anyway?

783

I am proud to be able to state that there are no mistprints
in this work –

# West Åland

*or*

Five Tombeaux for Mr Testoil

# *One*

1

Oh, the barmaid who, for the customers sordid benefit
*(O Lord, forgive me for what I am about to do!)*
what should I say
what say
what?
what? what?
who?

are you perhaps talking to me?
eh?
oh, do excuse me, my mind
went a complete blank for a moment there
for a moment I was back in that bloody bank

what else: spank tank clank drank flank prank lank yank
no, none of these will quite do
particularly not the last
ah well
unring the bell
canto
*grazie tanto*
better have a new beginning I suppose
and restore the experience in a different form

which some would presume to call a different experience
which is to say an end turned on its end to breed
since what we call the start is frequently the beginning
and what we call the beginning is frequently the middle
as is even more frequently what we call the end
and sometimes it seems to be over even before it has started
at the conclusion where commencement finds its centre
round the back of what is in fact the front

what do you mean I've come to the wrong place mate?

is anyone ever, in a sense, in the wrong place?
or, in another sense, ever anywhere else?

No. Let those who wish to micturate
in the River Plate and call it Destiny
or, if they prefer, Fate
do so by all means
for I have other plans

oh, the barmaid who removes the husk from the seed
for the benefit of her few more trustworthy customers
whom one's higher self could never quite trust even so
all of them being members of that suspect sex
which has a greater propensity for abstracted thought
and for exploding in pus during the long night

drifting in to their feeding grounds
from a life that must dismay them
almost as much as the thought of it dismays me
not even for a very good dinner I regret to say
with their unremarking nor too remarkable lusts
to the dimly lit, dank, doleful *Star and Anchor*
but which star, and which lightening, and which anchor?
lightning thundering and thundering in the empty house
though I dare say we need not ask, which dole
as I pointed out at least once when discussing the Whole
over the lemon sole with Ernesto Che de Altzpflegenheimer-Smith
whom I happened to fall in with
looking rather shabby
in a public convenience near the Westminster Abbey
insofar as there can be such a thing as a public convenience
(something profoundly public yet also profoundly convenient)
a good friend of the late Archbishop of Canterbury
as the 'photo' on the mantelpiece likewise urbanely suggested

we stood together down a deep hole
anguishedly discussing the soul
either that or the sole
near Knole

A GOD'S BREAKFAST

even I myself have often called there for a quick crepitation
caught short between the site of hidden domestic expulsions
which provide a rank metaphor for our own expulsion from Paradise
even if not quite of the first rank *heur heur heur*
(for in any perturbed suburb of sense
the mind grows squalidly witty in sheer self-defence
nor does it disdain another blossom for its hair)
*mais que fais-tu, ma belle et admirable fleur?*
*o, cueillez les fleurs mais ne vous faîtes pas jardinière*

which is always one way of putting it I suppose

it usually is

and the extremely satisfactory *maison de crapaud*
just off my office, devoted to my own more serious applications
such as, for instance, avoiding my first wife,
to whom I dedicated my poem of Christian conversion
shortly before I ran away and she killed herself
or who merely tried to kill herself did she
*cette espèce de chose*
and who, quite frankly, was off her head
anyway
though it is hardly for me to say
that such or such a one would be better off dead

she woke me out of a deep dream
deeper than I had known before
with its cargo of rapists and Mr Peacock
oh no wait a minute
to claim I was farting in my sleep
behaviour which I seriously deplore
and yet so like the woman
she tempted me and I did cheat
oh I don't doubt but I occasionally snore
though I forget most of the details

*(listen! o, listen!*
*what is that in the distance?*
*there came a sound of farting uncontrollably by night!*
*such an insult to our underwater existence.)*

though it is also more or less where I met my second
*insgesamt mit* its inspiring pictures of Joyce Mussolini and Dante
staring at each other with the wary mutual respect
of people who can speak Italian even better than I do myself
*mai dov'è la stagione, Signior Malvoglio?*

there I pondered the latest successes of European versification
if there is such a place as Europe, and such a thing as verse,
such as (to give but one instance) that magnificent hymn
*On Being Thrown Out of a Maison de Plaisir in the Place des Abbesses*
*Because of the Unbearable Whoops of Joy One Was Producing*
by that Transylvanian chap who used a pseudonym
whatever happened to him?
turning over a *pagina* oder *dva in* the latest *foglio*
or, rather more often, their abject failures

and sometimes ending the abasive act with a discreet cough
*(let us end all our abasive acts with a discreet cough)*
to extract my *Urschutzengel* from his latest moistened dream
of poisoned steams streaming off that large lake south of Munich
where so often you used to saunter in your curt *Parzefal* tunic
o my incomparable inamorata
for all the world as if our dramas
must be played out under Fujiyama
*(or some Fujiyama or other at least)*
whistling in bleak counterpoint a few of the leading themes
and I first realised my teeth were killing me

but not from heat; not heat; no; rather, frigor

nor as the sacred loss which shatters all of us
bit by
but by
bet by boat
by battalion
for the rough rapscallions
on their raw stallions
have outstripped all our stately galleons
which perhaps was only much as one might have expected

A GOD'S BREAKFAST

or like the flat slates that fall from the church's roofs
onto a passing procession of smug Prussian agnostics
who, it may well be,
had lately returned from an outing to Schiehallion
or some such place
where man once tried to estimate the proper weight of the earth
and, needless to say, failed


2

the religious mind, which is to say
what some people prefer

religious argumentation, which is to say
statements, whether solemn or angry (or both)

the enemies of God, which is to say
people I disagree with

but I am admittedly not quite infallible
whereas you are wrong about nearly everything
and he is St Thomas Aquinas

or, possibly, Kierkegaard

how much, nonetheless, I should like to thank her,
sitting, surrounded by three watchers, beneath a potted plant
possibly of *camellia japonica*
if there is such a thing
but unquestionably sitting there anyway

for if Shakespeare had been set to writing scriptures
lord, who would not believe
who would not believe they dropped to earth from the night sky

you know, I might even be tempted to believe myself
though I doubt if his opinion about a virgin who gives birth
was quite the same as mine

but then, few of us are entirely accurate about birth

for I have a warm, unsuspecting nature
whereas you are quite ridiculously gullible.
and he *(alas)* is a Roman Catholic convert


3

so we sat together in a small yellow tent
discussing what it all meant

though there is something so demeaning about mere meaning
one might leave that to one's servants or one's students
as one reads vintage car number plates for personal messages
I mean, I probably know I'm not doing it
unless I've managed to bamboozle myself as well
but do they
one rather doubts it
why else would they keep looking for what isn't actually there

for all the highest meanings are in the end unintelligible
and usually in the beginning too
since nothing which clearly means anything is transcendental
that much at least is self-evident. And therefore
to sound as if one is dealing in the transcendent
one has to sound obscure. It is sound business practice.
And if there's one thing I know something about, it is surely that

Therefore those extraordinary shifts and elaborations
in order to disguise the routineness of the thought
by adding to it the resonance of imprecision
the resonance of a resonant redundancy
we who think we can transcend a universe
of which we understand virtually nothing
but no doubt we do so with infinite humility

and the verbal dexterity also provides
(should such a thing be needed)
a justification of one's own good faith
the promise of an impending dawn of sense
a little delayed by now
week after week let's say

A GOD'S BREAKFAST

which is one of the advantages of meditation
over mere argument or explanation or exposition

it's all far too difficult simply to say what it is
so one releases a warm terrific wash
of yes words from the district's major conceptual systems
and everyone can sense a profound importance somewhere
somewhere around here, it must be somewhere around here
a vast meditative weight though no-one can locate
precisely where this profound importance may lie
(it is precisely far too deep to be located *precisely*)

I would say more but I can't find the relevant notebook
*(damn)*

for it is so difficult to get at the truth
so very difficult indeed
a truth more profound than mere 'facts' could ever be
in the sort of quintessentially superficial truth
which 'science' is forever throwing up in our faces
with its forms or its formats or its formulae or whatever
trite and misleading formulation they prefer
so how much wiser then are they
who give the appearance of getting at it in silence

pointless to ask to be given an example,
however slight, of a truth which cannot be stated in words
and too easy (again so like the scientist)
to talk of yet one more
of the apparently innumerable dishonest human attempts
to line up how things actually are
behind how one would like them to be
for whatever no doubt inadequate reason.

Which is why some have recourse to the tarot pack, I suppose,
with its pied and sympathetic over-simplifications:
the Winker *the Mug* the Gull *the Barefaced Shameless Liar*
the Man of God disappearing into the Bushes with a Tart
*the Cretin* the Failed Gigolo *the Con Artist*
the Unemployed Actress Who Can Hardly Believe Her Luck
*the Idiot* the Liar for Truth
and *the Man Who More than Once Lost His Wig at Sea*

oh it was a *British* sailor
came sailing home from France
and he had with him in his trunk
Napoleon's underpants

though some claim he was using them for a sling
but I dare say we all know what happened next anyway
during the full flowering of the Christian insanity

what?
oh I beg your pardon
what was I thinking of
a moment of routine inattention
this sort of mere abuse is unforgivable
how thoughtless no I meant to say
during the full flowering of the rank weeds of rationalism
there who could argue with that

*et in the Caledonia Road ego*
rather long ago now
*confiteor tibi Deo*
while the salt sea drifts away-o
towards St James's Park
which nowadays I tend to avoid in the dark
as did, or so I deduce, that inestimable saint himself

there me old Dutch used to buy her prunes and sago
*(which is also in some respects the blood of the shorn lamb)*
from an obscure cosmopolitan named, I believe, Diego,
a man much balanced in the hands of God,
who after an assault of the Chrestian runes
bedazzled the local seers

and a few hundred passing cross-country skiers
then was untimely washed ashore
to be reborn in New Amsterdam
but had possibly never so much as leafed through La Rochefoucauld
being (or so he said) an heretical martyr to lumbago
*grazie, prego*
*it'll be extra if you want me to clean out your ears* –
I am indeed what I am
not what I am
wham bam
*quel mélodrame*

me and the present King of Siam
who is (I am told) quite hilariously bald
even more so than the ninth symphony of Sibelius
which I have more than once seemed to hear in that silence
which lies behind the merely materialistic silence of the radio

hello hello
Jermyn Street calling
unreal
man

not that I found it particularly uplifting –
yet it passed a little of my time here on earth, I suppose,

if this is indeed mere earth, and if you can call it life
stuck in the bloody Fabber and Fabbro offices all day
writing or reading drivel in my swivel chair
weeping over returns or my tax returns
or rewriting or rereading for instance
*An Humble Megalomaniac Looks at His God*
(not one of my better efforts I'm afraid
though for some reason I nonetheless let it be published –
but then, they never are, are they?
being largely composed from bits left over in a wastepaper basket
but from what from the creation of the world?)

or somethings by Auden who I think we may all agree
certainly made nothing happen himself
though no doubt they were a powerful contribution
to the history of spirituality –
and, indeed, of masturbation in general

and if there also really is such a thing as time
and not just something else which behaves exactly like it
(for I would so much rather not place things in time
not just at the moment anyway
where it deplorably gets in the way of the rhetoric)

*de la rhétorique avant toute chose*

rather than a sublime sort, say, of transcendental custard powder
running to left and right while we examine the mental centre
as if it might be where the Master left the mustard of life
*(for how else designate*
*the reasoned seasoning of Time on Fate,*
*me old china plate?)*
and I am not just imagining all that is
which, frankly, I do sometimes rather wonder about

as, eheu, does my chartered accountant, Hugh, if he tells the truth
lifting his head to do so from a cryptic acrostic
of particular ferocity, or perhaps a filthy postcard
containing more limbs than seem absolutely necessary
such as I often shuddered over at Memphis in my youth
if I was ever really young

for I have seen some strange mistakes on the birth certificates


4

time travel is *(alas)* simply impossible
except, as it always is, now, travelling through time
in a forward direction, which direction is itself time
not some variety of time which merely happens
to be moving forward and forward and further forward
for it moves neither back nor off to either side

as the music which cannot be heard is not music at all
(I am not talking here about incidental effects)
and the music that seems timeless to listen to
requires time for it to exist as music in the first place

for time passes whether we notice it or not
it does not stop passing when we, enthralled
in something or in nothing, cease to notice it passing.
our minds too are part of a process, which is to say, of time

yes, truly; even our minds
which find it thrillingly easy to construct
impossible phrases such as 'existing outside time'
which is to say, existing outside existence

for the moment stressed with feeling anywhere in life
however joyful however apparently timeless
is still happening in time. The clocks continue to tick.
the heart pumps, the processes of digestion
continue on their disgustingly physical way
unobserved, unthought of, underestimated
but slowly changing internally onwards all the same.

and even our finest thoughts and feelings
require what Lucas would call metabolic processes
that is to say, changes – which require one might say time
or one might also say which are almost a synonym
for time, which is merely a calibration of changes,
which might perhaps be called a shorthand term for change

a feeling of timelessness as of anything else
can happen only in time, one might almost say
is itself time passing. For time is not a venue
in which other things happen. Only by unchangingness
only by a total static conformity
could time be conquered. A rather pyrrhic conquest,
you might say. And with no-one there to enjoy it

time is not an illusion, and even if it were
everything in the universe would be transient anyway

for only in time can time be imagined to be conquered

much as the birdbox
topples from the old wall down
into the wet lane

*oh, gorgeous impossibility of rococo cathedrals!*

for we shall not cease from exploration
and the end of our exploring
will be much the same as the end of anything else I suppose
which is to say, we shall quietly cease to exist
or quietly enough (if not as the tattooed buttock
which may be enlivened by a silent motto
perhaps the telephone number of the beloved
perhaps the not quite secret name of the Deity
perhaps a chorus ending from Euripides)
though the universe of particles I dare say will continue
or what we cannot do better than class as particles
since here at least words are chasing something
vastly strange to the world words were produced for and from
though as real a physical object as anything else.
As you, for instance. Or as the interstellar dust.

I sometimes wonder if that is what Attila the Hun meant.

It shall not be us at any rate. Not into light nor darkness
a disappearance merely, for a planet of dust
worries neither about planets nor about dust.

It does not ask if the dust was once a wall
or beings who turned other beings into stains on a wall
it does not, indeed, ask anything at all
it makes no remarks whatsoever
not even about the unreachable depths which surround it
for the worst of evil shall become an electric shimmer
nor does space ask questions, however allusively,
nor the clouds of debris hanker for the dull rock
nor the gorgeous civilisation, if there is such a thing

A GOD'S BREAKFAST

perhaps rather like a magpie on a tv aerial
or perhaps not
it flew away just there while I was looking at it
from what seemed like a very great height indeed


5

for what words may be made to do
the actual universe is under no compulsion
to follow, or even to acknowledge
whatever hoops we may cajole
our imagined world to squeeze itself through

yet all shall be well and all sorts of things shall be well
as the parachutist said before he disappeared down the well

*for in the end we will sit round a table in heaven pissing ourselves*
from motives which must at present necessarily remain mysterious
while the angels try to keep up with us as best they can

*Dear nuns, God drowned you because he loved you so much*

Yet I have always felt that if I had to urinate into a river
I should rather prefer it to be the Mississippi
for reasons which lie on the face of the facts, I suppose

Or one might perhaps wish to consider the universe a shared act
of quintessentially generous divine self-stimulation

which has now reached the stage of being commented upon
by various leading prestigious academic halfwits

of course the entire universe is rather a disappointment
rather a disenchantment to a man of my calibre

or as God might say, with an infinitely wry smile
*I can't believe I could have been as stupid as that*

though I have not sunk to depths of (I think) that rascal Pascal
who held that the entire universe was *au fond*
an act of gross intellectual perversity

or was that pederasty, I can never remember
which is which, though one tries one's best of course

*and Freedom shat herself when Wallace fell*

Oh, Shuvkin! Your wife was a silly tart! So what?
Was that a quite adequate reason for getting yourself shot?

and by the adopted son of a Belgian homosexual
apparently. Mind you, he was hardly a nice person.

which has been the epitaph of how many people by now
one rather wonders. gone gone gone gone gong
they have all f——ed off into a world of light

Yes. I sometimes wonder if that is what Jack the Ripper meant


6

in heaven there is no change, which is to say
there can be no such real life
no such life
for change is what real events are compounded from

as when, in St John's Wood
I threw louche parties in the nude
where leading ecclesiastics
and manufacturers of plastics
who did not give a toss
about St John of the Cross
to offer but one example
of which I could mention ample

mingled with their wives
having sheathed their dull knives
while the terror of outer space
lingered on every face

oh Your Eminence
pardon my vehemence
but some things must be said
before we're dead

and now that I have said them
excuse me
if I go off to bed
via the drinks cabinet

but is there still a stillness between the waves of the sea?
all sorts of waves elsewhere and everywhere
like the maddening little curves of my interpreters

or that chasm in Western history which may be called, the Church

But it's been nice meeting you.
And you. And you. And you anyway.
But, tell me, what will you do
when with a great roaring
a great flapping of wings
the Angel of the Lord
descends among the tea things
looking faintly bored
and addresses you all by name
from the middle of a sliding flame

Just asking. Good night.
Put out the light, and then
blacken your ashen faces and
put out the light again

amen

*o Lord, help us not to understand what we think we believe in!*
(it would be such a disaster to get too clear a view of *that!*)

let us gaze out forever at the darkening crescent
perhaps while listening to *the Wedding Present*

and when the sounds of the dustmen awaken me at ten
pardon my smile of content while I reach for my pen

much as a foreigner with extremely large testicles
might hide in the tiny grounds of a disused temple

though that is no doubt not an exact parallel
and I would not say that Jesus had a *particularly* successful life

for only through underpants can underpants be conquered
and in the end one grows tired even of that sort of thing

Yes. I wonder if that is quite what God the Father meant

I expect it was.

After all, he surely must have meant something. No?

Yes. One does rather like to think so.

# *Two*

1

alas the religious poet is beset by grave difficulties
wishing to expound the profoundest human thoughts
but hampered by the fact that his subject matter
for some incomprehensible reason, possibly
diabolic intervention, (if I may be forgiven
scratching these modern embarrassments) is such a quagmire
of human absurdity, wishful thinking and downright lies

thus one finds oneself willy-nilly forced to collude
in rambling on and on about things which do not make sense
intoning sounding absurdities in a solemn voice
as if one were somehow meditating one's way
closer to the truth, to a vast truth from beyond
spiritual truth which is no mere human meaning
but somehow the highest form of, as it were, failing to mean

which just happens to sound like more human absurdity

[I assume that should be *more* rather than *mere*, Ezra, no?
Not to worry. In any case it isn't *mire*, eh?
Har, har, har, har, har, har, har, har, har.]

It was, I think, F.H. Bradley who first pointed out
or was it perhaps Proust, I must check my notes
I dare say my secretary will gladly do it for me
(and not for the first time either)
that one should not feel prey to an existential shame
in moving towards vast meanings but never quite getting there
in committing oneself utterly, heart and soul,
to a gorgeous *mélange* of the vague, the self-contradictory
and the unintelligible
since to travel hopefully
is better than to arrive
jimi

oh, do forgive me
on closer inspection I find it was neither of them
life is not always as simple as it is
to the wise and ancient ecclesiastic who
perhaps in some leisure hour snatched from his solemn workings
might run his wet keen expert tongue repeatedly
over a bumpy, irregular but not unskilful image
of the Virgin Mary perhaps or Alice of Wonderland fame
insofar as the two of them are fit to be distinguished

yet still it is so easy to say to someone, so easy
to someone like myself for instance, so very easy
that obscurity is more often the absence of content
that your mystery is not particularly mysterious
but that viewed from elsewhere, as it were coolly,
it is merely *Unsinn,* clanging resonant nonsense
half-cocked self-satisfying confusions trumpeted
as being great truths beyond the bounds of reason
or the usual self-righteous, self-aggrandising pish

alas, alas,
for, to go no further,
something may be said for resonance, may it not
yes
yes, I think it may
I think it may
yes
prrrp
oh, excuse me
for the gaze riveted onto what lies beyond
there are difficulties everywhere

and one must also hum and stutter from time to time
to show that one is after all discussing immense profundities
for one would not wish one's impressionable followers
even in their fallibility to miss this important point

thus one meditates oneself into deeper and deeper awe
of a mystery which one has been unable to solve
(but of course one could not solve it, it's a mystery)
and since we are discussing the unfathomable

A GOD'S BREAKFAST

it is apt that our words should be unfathomable too
anything less would be a betrayal, a lapse
into the superficial – like science which, in its crudity,
seeks as it were to pull down the panties of the universe
despite its ever more desperate, anguished cries of
'I didn't mean it like that! You're not my type!
I require a more indulgent understanding!
They are an heirloom handed down from my mother!
You are misreading the signals!' Yes. And yet, not all of us
know that the oak is the acorn, the toddler the old man
lying dead in his oak coffin waving a bladder
while his brain disintegrates in a limited sense
rather like modern respect for the good, the true and the holy.

prrrrp
so terribly unreal
what?

yet, all these are necessary metaphors
for something immensely immense and other, which we
(though I scarcely mean that pronoun to coerce or intimidate –
no: one uses the first person plural impersonally
to avoid egotism, or at least the appearance of egotism)
which we cannot quite make sense of, which is to say,
cannot make sense of; symbols, I suppose we may call them;
symbols so profound, versatile and adaptable
that they have myriad uses, often simultaneously,
and are therefore not to be pinned down, to be limited
to any single referent. Rather, it seems they symbolise
more or less anything.

Yes. That is no doubt their strength.

and thus it is that melody, that the verbal music
can fill out in gorgeous tones the poor fallible thinking
the absence of clarity, the absence of mere exact meaning
which is somehow to be received as the intensest meaning
perhaps even beyond mere quotidian meaning itself

wheee

2

we have, likewise, the high-class tricks of language
since seekers after the ultimate rarely tire
of the suggestive paradox: that the main thing is to repeat
something one has never said before, and thus
as the picture might be restored but in a different form
so one must travel to where one already is
in order to meet oneself in the guise of the new person
which one once was, obscured by the glare of darkness
a darkness which, and so on and so forth till the hand
grows weary with the effort of repetition

after all, what else should the ultimate truth be
but something which sounds superb and eludes our comprehension?

Ah, how deep it is if even I can make no sense of it!
Dear Christ! It's so deep we don't even know what it means!

*(Thank God hallucinations happen only to unbelievers.*
*But, after all, that is why they are unbelievers. No?)*

In short, verbal mesmerism, a hoping that the music
will be taken for elusive meaning, meaning so profound
it cannot be said, or cannot be stated clearly –
something (rather a lot) of the high-class confidence trick.
It looks and sounds the part – but then, it so often does.

*There is only the resonant fraud. Nothing else is our business.*

A perfectly judged chorale of subtle vagueness
combined with revered inaccuracies, musically expressed.
Who would have thought it? Oh, he seemed so plausible!
You mean, it isn't really what he claimed it was after all?

*The underpants of day fall down round the ankles of night*

but possibly that is neither here nor there

A GOD'S BREAKFAST

3

Of course one may read a pattern in any unsimple surface.
Some see a face in the full moon. I do so myself, in fact.
Often I find it very difficult *not* to see it.
Others discern a hare. Others, I think, a garden.
And no doubt those who have the appropriate knack
might even contrive to see some sexual content to it
whether masculine or female. Or, perhaps, both.

*O pale hermaphrodite of the night sky*
*distant, inferior relative of the sun*
*writhing about in a dark, invisible hammock*
*trying to escape the influence of* π

*which cannot in fact be done*

If nothing more were claimed than the seeing or making of patterns
one could hardly object, though one might not be much impressed.
But few suppose the face, the hare, the garden are really there.

Yet by all means tell me, if I am missing something.

*Tell me your daughters soft dreams and I might even reply*

4

Oh, numberless generations of eager students
who have not realised that the signposts, where they exist,
are often unreliable, have been turned the wrong way round,
or give mere names without corresponding places
but took for granted
an eventual unearthing of something wondrous,
a heap of priceless ultimates
to be shared with them from the expertise of the learned
perhaps also present with the light donnish joke
the hint that one has impossibly read everything,
and long ago at that, the deft and knowing aside
as if to be modest about absurdities
to allude to them in hints wry winks and guesses
somehow rendered them less absurd or oneself

less culpable for taking such ballocks seriously

but those ambiguities which the sage author
has sagely put in place are hardly to be resolved –
they are deliberate, resonant opacities
their ambiguousness is the core of what they are.
Indeed where, perhaps through inadvertence or over-confidence,
they risk an explicit answer, they are often clearly wrong.

No, the point is to let others thrash around and through them
as if they were deep exactitudes a little obliquely expressed
(no doubt as such great depth exacts)
supposing the lack is theirs if they cannot quite understand.

so we need feel no surprise if the sagacious author
rarely saw fit to adjudicate between
various thoughtful readings of his lines
provided they were held with adequate awe
since much of the point was precisely to generate such wonderment
could this be right could that be right is it here or there
the frisson of nearly being there almost almost in sight is
what gives the whole enterprise its quivering foundation

small wonder then that the hordes fail to excavate
the vast, priceless treasure. For it was never buried.
It was never buried in bulk and therefore cannot be unearthed.
Little more than numerous subtle outlines and indentations.
But I dare say one may turn up a coin or two
and, suitably encouraged, keep on searching for more,
certain that this must be the right site after all.
And perhaps someone else has also lost something there.

5

Hmm. I dare say the image is not perfect. No. It never is.
But why not consider its positive aspects relevant
and let the negative ones be safely laid at the door
of the inadequacies of human language itself?
Such, after all, is the usual etiquette in a case like this.

for so much of the novelty, the seeming originality
comes from taking delightfully patinaed old beliefs seriously
and then trying to doctor them
into unabsurdity and relevance
baptising one's fumbles
as an act of meditation
(so much more impressive than merely, say, *thinking* –
so rich and deep a process that only rank vulgarity
would ask it to result in something intelligible)

whipping up a resonant word from theological discourse
pentecostal numinous transcendent incarnation
*(how smart he looks, with that incarnation in his buttonhole!)*
when the project flags or runs into difficulty
to intimidate the ranks into respectful silence
which is not quite Rilke's infinite almost silence of God

but then, what is?

6

yes, for instant significance just add the word God here
or refer to that great darkness which we call the death of God
though we may call anything the anything of God
with as much accuracy as anything else

verbal effect after verbal effect
conceptual prestidigitation trading
as wisdom or truth – or something very valuable anyway
far beyond mere words, whatever it might be

after all, there have to be limits to human humility

and all these beautifully calculated evasions
these hints that we could pick up, if only we were
slightly more active, perhaps as alert as the author
or if only he had expressed himself ever so slightly differently
which he might well have done – but, as it happens, did not.

with occasional flamboyant
expansions of the supremely obvious
to show one's respect for the lowest rungs of meaning
though the other end of the ladder be however far in the clouds


7

yet what does so much of this immense wisdom amount to
when it condescends to show up within our range of vision?
an endless shovelling in of desperate excuses
for supposing that death is not what it quite obviously is

and often the sly revelation of –
well, we can't say of what
it is all far far too otherly for that
but we know it is most important and almost certainly
assures us that things continue after ceasing to exist


8

but that which is not being formulated in words
simply is not being *formulated* at all, is it?

or can truth be an anonymous wisp of feeling?

for what might an unformulated truth be?
it's too much I suppose to ask for an example

the opposite, perhaps, to an unformulated lie?

Or possibly by now this crude dichotomy of truth and lie
has been transcended? Might that be it? For it seems
one meets the most difficult points (or, rather, fails to meet them)
by proclaiming them transcended. One's favoured absurdities
cannot be absurd. No, no. They *transcend* reason.
All explicit objections must therefore miss the point.

Or are there also lies too great
to be enshrined in mere, approximate words?
It seems somehow mere prejudice
to suppose that greatness eludes us
in one direction only.

Perhaps it is relevant here that our sublimest concepts
go always *beyond* reason. That they never, say,
go below it or fall short of it. They never miss it
to one side or the other. Yes. That is certainly
some sort of consolation. One is at least consoled.

For words fail, but the meanings carry on
we are assured. Always exact. Always accurate.
Never, for instance, delusive.
Never elusive, never delusional. No.
Off in a sort of limbo, glowing beside their guarantees –
which are presumably wordless guarantees

for words may fail to communicate but still have meaning
and if one fails in the right way then these meanings
are incredibly great, though one cannot quite say what they are

and indeed the fact that the wisdom cannot quite be stated
is in itself surely the most impressive evidence
for it being a part
no doubt an important part of the profoundest wisdom of all

## Three

1

so here I sit, an old man with bad teeth, a prostate problem
and few remaining ambitions except to die suddenly

(ah, to die and at last be out of the grasp of dentists!
every one of them! every last gasping one of them!)

as one's whole life was spent with a vague sense
that it wasn't really happening, that something else
was happening in its place instead
through some curious lapse by the hidden supervisors

not much helped by this widespread insistence on talking
of certain quasi-ultimate human inventions
as if they were not human, came from somewhere else,
had always been there, even before the humans arrived

things hung together, that is the aspect that matters
as they must have done if we are to be here at all

glimpsing the milestones of decades with mounting disbelief
these sudden blessed moments of something or other
an ancient git whom life has mostly passed by
as one who well might say
*I came, I farted, I departed*
*I tried not to be too hard-hearted*
reading Petronius and hiding in convenient cupboards
from one's wife or one's ex-wife, as so many of us must do
or one's ex-wife's ex-husband for that matter
since that is what so many relationships seem to be about

as I dare say it passes so many of us by
the normality of lives sustained by outrageous fantasy
though *homo sum* and I therefore searched for the truth
and also the perfect womb, if there is quite such a thing
and I am not simply catching hold of the wrong end of the stick

A GOD'S BREAKFAST

for in the end everything is tolerable
except perhaps things as they are

hello, sailor
give me the name of your gaoler
has anyone ever told you you look like Jeremy Taylor
whoever he might be
the author of *Wholly Living* and *Wholly Dying*
unless I have been seriously misinformed
I really must get round to trying
to read it some day
perhaps you would agree to read it to me
what do you say
on a warm afternoon
somewhere down Warwick Way
where I used to stay
Good Lord, you're crying
do try to stop that
fairly soon
here's some money for a new harpoon

but I suspect sometimes that life is just too difficult
like the most useless subject one ever had at school
which in my case I suppose was something like arithmetic

and which some otherwise strangely untalented people
were yet so good at, surely much too good at
where did they get that undeserved flair from
who had been giving them lessons before they were born?

but here I am anyway, a mother's seventh and last child
brought out when she was already forty-five
a complete fluke, in other words
a rampant accident
something unmeant
clearly the youngest of the family
fifteen years younger than his earliest sibling
which is rather longer than most emperors managed to last
to others the unnecessary late and puking newcomer
having just, as it were, made it in through the closing gate
but nonetheless strangely ready to pontificate

some years after I had stopped befouling myself
on a daily basis, literally at least
and had picked up how to make more impressive noises

from exhaustion to self-hypnosis
from self-hypnosis to talking oneself to a standstill
in the rumty tumty tumty rumty tumt
yes something like that
the appropriate words should be in the dictionaries somewhere
on that shelf right beside me with a bit of luck
oh incomparable fake

I merely want time to stop. Is that too much to ask?

but okay it is still going
and here I am, an old man stripped to or from the waist
sitting with a dazed expression in a women's public library
wondering if this might be a misprint for lavatory
but surely not surely not. For that would be quite illegal.

But isn't the whole cosmos in some deep sense illegal?
Yes. I suspect it might well be.

Of course I could always plead confusion or desperation.

One so often does, in the course of a life, I find.

Obscurely in touch nonetheless with supernatural truth
a truth beyond mere human truth and falsity
(for is there a single room anywhere in the planet
where grotesque self-delusion has never flourished?
I hardly think so. And certainly not here.
Dear God, wherever else, certainly not here!)

banging on about how much one could say
very like the proverbial shithouse door
what great things if only mere human language
had not so comprehensively let me down again
(for the bearings on which existence runs
if it honestly might be said to run at all
are neither the balls of one's feet nor the spheres of outer space)

inventing a world of words, and then exploring the words
as if one were exploring the actual world
the world in which the derivative world of words was mocked up

still, there is little point in taking
the inadequacies of language personally
indulging the rather simple confusion that exploring
the meaning of certain words is equivalent to exploring
the meaning (as if there could be such a meaning)
of the universe as a whole. No, for the whole thing
cannot mean anything, since meaning derives
(though perhaps this is another sense of meaning)
from that which is unimportant or means nothing
compared to which the rest has the meaning it has.

Meaning derives from the other bits,
derives from the bits without meaning,
requires the existence of these less meaningful factors.

Yes. Listen. What? A totality simply *is*.
It means nothing. What can it signify?
It means nothing beyond itself. There is no beyond itself.
whatever you call the All, with a God or without,
there is nothing else to calibrate it against for significance.
Or, as it may be put, it transcends mere meaning.
In the light of what thing (what greater thing?
what greater thing could there be than the totality?)
could its meaning emerge; what could that be derived from?

whatever the All might be, that is all it is

and what words may be made to do
the actual universe is under no compulsion
to follow or even to acknowledge

Yes. I think that gets some of it really rather well.

Though, obviously, not all of it.

2

Because I have complete
Because I have
Because I have completely lost touch with reality

it being so crude and inadequate for my great purposes

Because I have learned to take the greatest fantasies seriously
and clothe myself in incense and talk about the beyond
as if I were talking about anything real
(if we must descend to such mere *technicalities*)

and have been terribly well educated into the bargain

I permit myself the occasional luxury
of attempting to draft 'a rough sketch – an *ébauche*' –
(presumably for those English-speakers who do not quite know
what the English word means, but who do recognise the French one)
entitled either *The Idea of a Christian Society*
or *Playing With Myself Quietly in the House of a Trusted Friend*

wherein I embark on such complex and vexed matters
as 'the grace of God without which human operations are vain'
(well now: how, without omnipotent grace, are they even *possible?*)
or 'reciprocal sacramental advantages for travellers'
(which is surely a gorgeous epitome of life as such –
besides being such a *wonderful* candidate for a high-class title)

much, some might say, like a retired senior civil servant,
or a superior, more adult version of the boy scouts

behaving like the gifted newcomer taking over the gang –
(but where did he come from? whence that funny accent?)
or the gifted new bully imposing himself on the fellowship
which he found *in situ*, as a natural leader of men

(since, after all, one once compared Villon to Heraclitus,
ostensibly offhand, which is hardly the sort of thing
a mere run-of-the-mill commentator would do, now is it?)

so, after years of playing the piano
in an exquisitely high-class brothel, exquisitely well,
one has by widespread consent been elevated
to the status of a genuine professor
with impressive strings of letters after one's name

and off one goes in a persistent fog of twittering and perhaps,
a *Gesamtkunstwerk* of learned, polyglot throat-clearing
interrupted by strong unargued *diktats* and *fiats*
with a great deal of 'It is not my intention here'
and 'I am not here concerned with', so that it seems
one is carrying on a discussion for page after page
entirely in terms of what it will *not* be about

since 'I am neither a sociologist nor an economist,'
(no, Magister; and the list could be greatly extended)
'and in any case it would be inappropriate,
in this context,
to produce any formula for setting the world right.'

(Indeed; indeed.
Always so important to do things in the proper context.
But we would so much like to hear this 'formula'
and so must pray he found the proper context for it elsewhere.)

Besides which, 'to aim at originality would be an impertinence',
and who wants to be impertinent
in such important matters as these anyway

so much *meta* fluff and noise everywhere
so much discussion of what the discussion should be about

('I have no first-hand acquaintance with the doctrines of Dr. Arnold,
and must rely upon Mr. Murry's exposition of them.'
Well, Master: you could also *read them yourself*, could you not?
Or would that be to take mere humdrum scholarship too far?)

until at last one painstakingly manages to suggest Z
often next adumbrating a real objection to Z
to which one perhaps replies by restating Z,
but this time much more stylishly, or with greater intensity
before assuming that this has somehow seen off the objection

yea, greater even than the sort of fulfilment,
if one is allowed to adapt a phrase from modern literature,
that the great man gets from a really successful shit

and so the straw men explode on every side
heads thrashed into chaff by this new Don

oh, the nude Don in the new dawn
who some thought was a mere dreamer
lets out another eloquent yawn
as he combats the crude blasphemer
on the greensward of prawn-coloured Old St Vaughan's
startling the soon-to-have-vanished swans

Adolphus put his life in pawn,
but when he went back for it, it was gone
so who was the Redeemer?
John?
Hello?

for 'It is a matter of concern not only in this country,
but has been mentioned with concern by the late Supreme Pontiff,'
(which one rather takes to be a reference to the Pope –
ah, who does not recognise here the voice of wisdom itself?
someone certainly concerned about the vital issues of our time)
'speaking not of one country but of all civilised countries,'
(one would rather like a clean list of these select countries)
'that the masses of people have become increasingly alienated
from Christianity' – since, without Christianity,
who could suppose them to have been truly civilised
in the first place? Ah, yes. Or, one more sparkling example:

'if our society renounces completely its obedience to God,
it will become no better, and possibly *[possibly!]* worse,
than some of those abroad which are popularly execrated.'
Hmm. Not execrated by the finer, purer minds,
from what I can see. No. *Popularly* execrated.
People like Hitler and Stalin, one rather assumes.
No better and possibly worse. Selah! That's telling 'em.
Oh, pluck your finely tuned instrument forever.
We seek your guidance. Or at least we like the noise.

'What is often assumed,' said the Master, 'and it is a principle
that I wish to oppose, is the principle of live-and-let-live' –
which is to say, between the Church and the State.

I grow stout… I grow stout…
I shall walk through St Paul's with my balls hanging out.

The main problem with religion is that some people take it so *seriously*.

And if the truth shall kill us, then we must make some hard choices.
Though it is hard to see how we could know this, and truth too can be hard
    to know.
And perhaps we might care to remember that we would all end up dead anyway.

Though, of course, it is also important not to overrate this mere fact either.

## *Four*

1

although I seem to be
although I seem
although I seem to be farting uncontrollably

nothing much else appears to be happening down there
but then, that is true of so much history in general,
isn't it? all that sound and fury, for what?

On Linden when the sun was low
There lay a huge metallic po
From which a dim uneasy glow
Announced the end of history

*oh grant us at least, o Lord, the consolation of hell,*
*which is to know that the worst has at last happened*

or have I already said that? One tries not to
repeat oneself to repeat oneself one tries not to

after all, one can get used to anything
within a broad range of life, except perhaps uncertainty

Many shall fart where many meet
Many shall whisper 'Life's a cheat!'
And every sod beneath their feet
Will be a bloody mystery

but the infant nonetheless always precedes the adult version
and old age, if it comes at all, always comes after these

this is so routinely and instantly obvious
that it requires great gifts for incantation
to render such things obscure or problematic; for instance
suggesting that time present, past and future
if there is such a thing as time present
or if there is any other sort, this three which is one
is or are wrapped up in two of Einstein's old vests

and are hidden somewhere or other, as so much might be,
in the old garden shed where my father used to work
which still is almost exactly as he left it
at his death nearly a decade ago, and where I
have spent, all told, not even an hour of my own life so far.

(Odd indeed. That crept through quite unexpectedly.
Much as Russian maidens used to emerge from the old *versts*,
with their mushrooms, their strangely moving turns of phrase
and their enduring hopes for happy, remoter weddings.)

likewise for the simple, obvious truth
that the past cannot be affected in any way whatsover
however our perceptions about it might change

how can the impossible be possible?
*it isn't*
how can the impossible have happened?
*it didn't*

stains on an old man's crotch
prompt dim memories of debauch
while the nearby savant raises
an eyebrow to the secret phases

of the (alas) light-hidden stars
and on Jupiter, Bute or Mars
the pattern of our daily fears
flickers, flares and disappears

and at night the daffodils
stand still beneath the streetlamp, next to
the boarded-up school


2

for lyricism can be a knack, much like anything else

and one recollects a few books that one read decades before
as an undergraduate (or that one did not quite read
but marvelled at from a distance) perhaps flicking through

some later discussion of them, by a distinguished fraud
plagiarist or halfwit very often; and one realises
that there was rarely really all that terribly much there;
not nothing, certainly, but rarely terribly much
not the glory, the burgeon, the excess, the had-to-be-grasped,
the bridge between two vast worlds, the great creative enterprise,
or even the large nun shouting 'f——!' in a reference library –
but rather another old fart with a good ear, trying his best
(at first I struck 'a good er' and I am loath to part with it)
and in the end not doing all that terribly much with it really.


3

for he is not dead, merely completely annihilated

only less and less ordered with every moment that passes
except for innumerable metaphorical senses

but what may not be given a metaphorical life
even the white plastic bag that blows down the street
until a low branch or a clever arm catches it

for the complex body was a complex person
and the complex body rots or is destroyed
which is what the person was, much like the next person

Look! Look! How many do you see up there?
Do you see one person or only three?

and how much deader do you have to seem to be
in order to be acknowledged as having ceased to exist?


4

Of course we are all inadequate. The cosmos is inadequate.
As indeed was the fare at the *Cosmos* restaurant
and the films shown in the *Cosmo* cinema.
It may be seen as an infinite inadequacy.
And so we continue to talk to ourselves and call it God.

These revered acts by which the over-optimistic
seek to communicate with the non-existent
and hear a wild spectrum of imaginary replies

unlike a priest who might see a former beloved face
in the congregation and hurry through the requiem service
to take her off to a hotel room and, with luck, have sex with her

which I vaguely remember reading about in a newspaper recently
perhaps in a hallway in Holloway, Galway or Delft,
or a room in the only decent hotel on Iona
where even the typically insensitive atheist
has to fight like a spiritual Jonah
according to Doctor Samuel Johnson
which is to say, in a certain sense, myself


5

*Since Love commands me, Madam, to stick this thing in here*

Oh, all right, so I decapitated the cat.
It was whimpering in a philosophical nightmare.
What else was I supposed to do about that?
Could I, I wondered, possibly be dead already myself?

A St Bernard is a dog. A chihuahua is a dog.
And a dog is, obviously, a dog. And therefore
a St Bernard is a chihuahua. QED. Woof.
Do you tell me you are looking for even greater proof?

oh, you who say in loud voices in the Underground
*People are listening to me, but I don't care*
why not give them the chance not to listen to you
are we in the cosmos only on the rebound

voices seep into my room from the street from the hallway
from the room above from the room to the left to the right
often I do not know where the voices come from

which is surely, in its way, entirely appropriate
for I believe it says, somewhere in the *Dhammapada*
though I make no explicit claim to have the whole work at my fingertips

and perhaps I possibly mean the *Bhagavadgita* anyway
or the *Rig Veda,* which is no doubt not quite the same thing,
or might it even be the *Lakantavara Sutra*

or the incomparable patrology of Father Migne
or somewhere in Rumi or the Angelic Doctor
or Jerome or Augustine or the Talmud or Sigmund Freud

or for that matter *The Man With Two Left Suspenders*
which was rather a *succès d'estime* in my youth
(for statistics shyly suggest that I too was young once)

not all of which I have read quite from beginning to end
but somewhere or other anyway we hear them or hear of them
coming at us from all directions at once
many of them delusive, many wheedling
many of them not particularly addressed to ourselves
nor, one sometimes suspects, to anyone else either
and that we must try to hear what we can, as best we can
and make the best answers we can to what we hear
and communicate as best we can with those about us
adapting oneself as best one can to the reality about us
as one might perhaps turn wearily round on the tree-trunk
to the whimpering wreck beside one, and enquire
whether by any chance he had a spare cigarette
accepting without demur the brand he limply offers
despite the fact that it would by no means be
one's own first choice, but in the circumstances
prepared to compromise, surrounded as one is
by physical beings to whom the straightforward thought
that that is what they are, physical beings,
seems too much to grasp, too graspable to be true;
and all the subtlety they are capable of shows
what subtlety the physical is capable of
rather than that they are something else entirely
too subtle to formulate. To whom the process
(the most simple of all, perhaps therefore called miraculous)
of giving birth comes almost as a surprise
a strange descent into blood and physicality
from our so elevated spiritual normality,

A GOD'S BREAKFAST

surely we should arrive here in a somewhat less basic manner?

we who between routine evacuations
let our wild minds flourish about the supernatural
which is to say, the impossible, the unreal
that which cannot quite exist but does so so bewitchingly

for since very few of you are cunning writers yourselves
you will scarcely be able to know from the inside or guess
what the production of rhetoric is or fiction;
that there are techniques for this as for so much else
and that those who have the technique
can seem to be doing the impossible
to those who lack it. All that time devoted
(well, we must pass the time somehow, I suppose)
to the single, priceless untraceable treasure
which isn't there, about or behind the universe.

For there is nothing behind the universe.
It is not a veil, or a covering, or a lid.
As simple or as complex as it is
it is what is, and we are spared the sad task
of asking what lies behind what lies behind what lies behind it
or what lies beyond that or to the side of it
or what lies behind that or behind that or in front of that
for the end of our beginning is the opposite
of the start of our commencement. So let us finish
with a hymn, or at least with a peace of resonant mumbling
which some might consider merely a piece of resonant mumbling,
something which lasts at any rate for long enough
to convince ourselves and others that we at least
have expended a power of time in searching for an answer.

But which hymn should we sing? There are so many possibilities.

Are there not always so many possibilities?

Or at least the delusion of so many possibilities
which must come to much the same thing

So which hymn should it be?
Should it be: I *Can See The Vast Light In His Ears*?
Or *I Managed to Get Rid of One of My Three Eyes This Morning*?
Or that old favourite, *Two Fried Eggs and an Invisible Penis*?

Oh, Mister Othello/Was a very stupid fellow.
He took the life
Of his delightful if somewhat naive wife.
And his favourite colour was a bilious yellow.

Does that help much? No. No, I hardly think so.
But a rich choice remains to us yet.
What of *Further Adventures Among the Biscuit Worshippers*?
Or *Real Life Is Not Many People's Speciality*?
Or shall it even be, *The Sanctity Professionals*?
May it be so?

No; no; no. no.
Let us approach our task with all due cretinity.
To the tune of *April, That Most Delightful of Months*
Let us open our mouths anyway and see what trickles out
No doubt it will be much the same old story.

'Tis surely (*Madam*) not for me
To pull thy tites about;
Nor scream 'I think I need a phee!'
Whene'er the lights go out.

No! Life ordains both time and place
For all its joys and woes.
Because she parted in my face
Must we be *deathless* foes?

Yes

You know, I sometimes wonder
if that is not what the Blessed Oderic of Pordenone meant.

And did he ever reach Shangrila, I wonder?

Yes. I for one do rather hope so.

A GOD'S BREAKFAST

# *Five*

1

All right. The whole thing is too ridiculous for words.
One has now lived longer than Shakespeare. And as one ages,
the great minds of the past seem to flounder more and more.

How clearly they are merely large mammals trying to do their best
and as for future great minds, if any,
they are surely such an astonishing irrelevance

Odd all the same, isn't it, how we are born
how we grow up (at least in a manner of speaking)
kid ourselves on for decades, then plummet from the perch
having brought much the same confusion to other people
many of whom no doubt were even children of our own.

oh cousin Hughie
from St Louis
had an affair with a deepsea buoy
and never trusted the water again
isn't that so like men

*et in Arcadia fui*

in the words of the well-known popular song
or one which was at least popular a long time ago
which I quote merely to show that I too have lived

and who better then than I to take you on a tour
of the ineffable, the fundamentally
unsayable, the inexplicable, that which
passes mere human potentiality of thought?

moaning exquisitely onwards, almost saying things
almost making sense, even if others insist
that deftly moving the ancient creaking mental furniture about
is not in itself great thought
but there are ways, are there not,
of fabricating significant cogitation

to wit, God and time and resonant English placenames
such as might enchant the visiting American
with a reference thrown in to St Paul or St Augustine
to heighten the tone – St Paul of Tarsus that is,
for who are we to doubt that such a person existed,
not St Paul, Minnesota – and certainly not St Louis;
no, let us ignore St Louis. Yes, even, alas, he
who brought back the original crown of thorns
to the awe of those who in his saintly palaces
had hitherto sat contemptuously playing with their phalluses
but now instead the cramped cupolas rang
to the paeans which they thus over-carefully sang

Who broke the pantry window? *Love.*
Who whispered through the keyhole? *Hate.*
Who thinned the study out? *The Dove*
*Which cut the laughing throat of Fate.*

Who kicked aside the rusted gate
Of prejudice and silent pride?
*The hermit who was not inside*
*The tomb we wished to desecrate*

for o Lord, remember me
when you come to portion out your blessings
among that sex which has the greater propensity
for reading maps and urinating into bottles
with or without expressions of superhuman intensity
and whether or not at the same time

2

and who might you be to doubt that I am purveying
superhuman truths? Pull down your underpants!
Er, no, sorry – I mean: pull down your arrogance!
Honestly admit that I am far over your head!'

of course there are people who disagree with me
but deep down they are just completely effing wrong, okay?
they just don't have my ineffably inexplicable subtlety, okay?
though of course one forgives them, since they know not what they do to one

worship likewise a God who created us because of his love
for his as yet non-existent creatures to whom
he then gave such a hard time, because he loved them

for too many things ostensibly manifest poor design
like a bedside lamp or, perhaps more disagreeably,
the ramshackle blundering universe which contains it
and so many other small lamps, whether lit or unlit

but what of that?
life concentrates when the land is flat
only non-existence is totally free

and when my darling shows off her modest titles to me
I thank Almighty God, that well-known sexual maniac,
that I was born with seminary vesicles

they are called seminaries, I suppose,
because they are awash with seamen?
but one may talk with an imaginary God anywhere

so by all means
let's sing a raucous shanty
of Captain Maginty and co
curiously reminiscent of Cavalcanti
to those in the know
for I have mislaid my soul in a pile of papaya beans

after all, we are fairly near the river down here

Oh, and by the way,
how is the health of your indomitable Auntie?
her with the perplexed mien
and the home-made perspex screens
Fanny, or whatever the fur and faex she was called

*(which is merely another way of saying, death)*

(Still, I suppose I may at least claim I did it all myself)

What, mate? You married a flat-chested wife
*(I heard a voice within the tavern say)*

and yet you presume to give me advice about life?
You'll go too far some day, you know

oh Shah Jahangir
had a mighty whanger
he parked it in an aircraft hangar
then ran off to the appropriate office for a licence
though getting a valid one in a hurry isn't all that easy, it seems,

*for the universe is not as good as it ought to be*

such optimism can be revealing
and often not unappealing
if you want to know my considered feelings
in this rather arcane technical matter

and yet that is not why
when at dead of night
I get up for a –
for what I should here like to call
an occasional late flight
which is not to be thought of as the type of dreams
I often intuit an uncanny presence
drifting in from the *Schottenanger*
and conjuring up a quite impossible *frisson*
among the brittle, fevered, forgetful chatter

which I expect is a profound metaphor of some sort
perhaps for the place of faith in this godless world
or possibly vice versa

3

for it is exactly as if one were to be asked
what is the secret what is the great secret
tell us if you or anyone else can the greatest of all secrets
what is, let us say, the name of the capital of Nepal
but for God's sake inform me without referring to Katmandu
under any designation at all

assuming they don't now go ahead and change it
doubtless in a spirit of sheer ideological perversity

A GOD'S BREAKFAST

*though it can often be such a relief to think it is all over*

but no-one can do it can he
why are we so powerless
for I much prefer that word
to the one my ex-ex-wife so rudely favours
that she beats it crudely out
on the kitchen table in demi-semi-quavers
to one of Gustav I. Straina's *Songs For Swinging Pederasts*
insofar as my untrained ear can quite interpret the call
among all that clatter of savage cutlery

thus, tell me what happens to me when I have ceased to exist
it's such a mystery isn't it
but do so without saying that I shall have ceased to exist
give me any other answer but that

tell me the truth, but not if it means
telling me the raw truth
yes, that is my sole proviso
that is the single restriction which I would wish to impose
tell me, for instance, the cube root of twenty-seven
without in any way referring to the number 3

I mean to say, that's only what it looks like
is there some other method for being really dead
and yet how we do know something impossible
isn't happening instead

for how appropriate it is that the secret name
the secret name of the Lord as it has been conceived
should mean merely existence (if such indeed it does)
since existence in itself of course does not exist

except in the world of concepts, itself a concept
along with the verbal swarms of other squawking concepts

*for there is nothing indestructible within us*

and how ridiculous other people are nonetheless
with their absurd opinions, hopes and holes

from all of which they testify unceasingly to their Gods

*Oh, come on, there are more people waiting in the queue*
*than (if I may say so) you —*

whispered a shrill dull voice from the still crowd
another warm skull rolling from the field of skulls
who had skilfully unmanned himself for stark personal reasons
during a blinding performance of *A Fake Tan For All Seasons —*
oh God, yes, the theatre —
I had almost forgot —
you say *castrahto*, I say *castrayto*
but both of us by now do somewhat despair of Plato
all the same

though one admits it's a rather charming name

even if he was, alas, like Aristotle, an heathen


4

Or might it have been another play entirely
*The Cock and Tool Party*, perhaps, or some such charade
by an ageing purveyor of high-class balls to the gentry.

Oh, can I ever forget those triumphs of my last years?

Eternally the finest moments ricochet between my ears:

*— But my dear, there was no hippo. Didn't you see that?*
*That was what made the whole thing so f——ing funny. Another gin?*
*This new flat is full of spirits, of one sort or another.*

*— And then what happened, when the bells had stopped ringing?*
Did the ghosts, or whatever they were, disappear at once?

*— Well. I was in my study, you know, in Foxhall Mansions,*
*Being whipped with a wreath of thorns by my late wife, Faith —*
*You've met her, Clive; latterly she had been training*
*For a post as a tax evasion advisor in Tunbridge Wells —*
*Where St Alban grew his head back on, remember? —*

When, in a blinding flash, brighter than any searchlight,
The spirit of the Lord must have descended upon me
And I befouled myself and passed out. The usual story,
In short. Can you forgive me? When I came to,
(If one can ever truly be said to come to)
I was serving seventeen years without the option
For burglary, or was it buggery, something like that,
In a place with the charming name of Albany,
Which almost certainly I did not as such commit.
No. My passport clearly states I was abroad at the time.

– Not in Albania, Hugo?

– No; not in Albania,
Unfortunately. In Jerusalem, as it happens.
Where would we be without that fearfully gifted city?
Do not enquire what my occult business there was.
But let us get one thing straight. It had nothing to do with armaments.
Nothing to do with armaments; nothing to do with money;
And nothing to do with anything in between. All right?

– As for myself I shall take the wise precaution
Of leaving through this window, shot sideways out of a cannon.

– Or could that possibly be, shot out of a 'cannot'?
For life, they tell us now, is a sort of misprint. No?

Unless perhaps you have a trampoline available, Sir James?

– No, I have not revisited the East since half my face was gnawed off.

– And not even the right half, that's somehow the most terrible thing.

– Enough! We must make the best of a bad job, Cordelia.
We must not despair. There is always hope for all of us.
For me especially, of course. But also for you too.
Even for you, and the likes of you. Yes. For God
Is quite astonishingly merciful, when it comes up his hump,
As they used to say in the Army. Intelligence Corps, of course.
Ah, those dear old army days! Have they ever yet worked out
What must have happened to the dismembered mascot, I wonder.

– The rabid camel? No. It worried me more
To observe the inflated antennae still shuddering around me.

– *Oh, some things are just so difficult to say, aren't they?*
*Try reading the Kabbala if you don't believe me.*
*But be careful not to give away the ending.*
*About the ultimate mysteries, one can never quite be silent enough.*

– But to what does this lead? Or, rather: what is this leading to?

– *It ran out from under that cupboard and disappeared under this bed.*

– Can you hear someone snoring? *Might it not be all of us?*

But no one deed or thought was ever all of us, was it?

*so: kindly put aside that overworked kazoo*
*and teach us to distinguish the less from the lesser*
*o relatively objective and literate Professor*
*Or do you*
*perhaps mean to stay in there all day*
*pray*

Yet, how can one stay all the time anywhere?
Oh bless her! Bless her and bless her!
(Garblimey! These stains are going to take a power of shifting.)
But it was not, as I said to the Lord, something I had ever planned.
No. It was not.
And one is rather tired sometimes of being such a one-man band.

*For one noise, I dare say, is much the same as another;*
*whether it starts a universe or finishes it.*

For why, Lord, should there be nothing rather than nothing?

nothing, nothing, no, not, *Not*

And can there even be silence, my Lord, when there is nothing?

# *What Else Is There?*

120 Poems

## Preserving the Moment

Look! There is the poet's original manuscript.
There are some dark marks where (perhaps) a droplet of tea was spilled.
And there are some lighter marks, caused perhaps
by a few stray drips when the plants were being watered.

And look there! On the reverse side of the paper
there is an invitation to a wonderful-sounding party
which took place fifty-odd years before the poem was written.
The poem? Oh, yes. Yes. There was a poem there too.


## I Had Hoped It Wouldn't Be Me

Ah yes. The biography. The autobiography.
The remote ancestor who once met a head of state,
or was patted on the head by some vaguely remembered genius.
The unforgettable garden which housed the forgotten childhood.

In another room, the first significant new meeting.
The work which surely showed a quite astonishing maturity.
Friends who will scarcely be written about. A sad loss.

A batch of baffling children, soon to swell and disperse.
Work after work, expanding beyond so many boundaries.
A minor health worry. The now automatic respect.
A reputation slowly taking root in foreign countries.

Success. Mature reflections. What? A routine trip to hospital.
What? Death, or the death of an irreplaceable second.
Kind words from one's keenest enemies. Dispersal.
The first appearances in the worthwhile encyclopaedias.

The mistaken detail. The inaccurate résumé.
The electrical edge which cuts through inner space.
Death again. The subtle dust falling onto the planet.
The subtler universe drifting on through the dust.
And the much less subtle dust, or whatever one wants to call it.

# The Inheritors

Opening the cupboard which had remained locked
for the greater part of a century, they found there –
well: what was it they found there, Sir? A key?
A potted plant? Did a bullet come flying through?
Or a spear? No. No; of course not. Did a dog fall out?
No; not as such. Nor a frog. So: what then *did* they find?
Oh, a few old letters thrown in a box. A single worn shoe.
And a bundle of cloth on the uppermost shelf, which contained
enough small bones to make a very nice little skeleton.

So they threw everything out without inspecting it
all that closely. Everything but the letters.
These, they took from the box, sat down at a table
and began to read. And, by God, they were boring!
There was nothing whatsoever of interest in any of them.

## 4

Who, indeed, wants the stars to contain literary critics?
I know one who lives in this street, and one is enough.
One critic, that is. We say hello now and then.
Or sometimes I say hello, and he fails to answer me.

## 5

Something with *far* too many legs running along the windowsill!
Quickly! I pick a copy of Antony Flew's *Merely Mortal?*
and clobber the bastard to death. Good! That's so much better.
Phew. Where would I be without my library books?

## Passing Through

Narrowly avoiding a leisurely attempt to squash it,
the fly flew out of the window, between various pillars,
and off into the wilds beyond. It settled on
various slabs and sundry heaps of excrement
from one source or another, before descending
for a second or two of rest at the filthy circumcised penis
of a naked grunting man who was being crucified.
It crawled a little way round towards his seeping buttocks,
found, perhaps surprisingly, nothing there to detain it,
and flew up onto his head. The head was still alive.
It stayed there for a while, gathered a little nutrient,
completed one or two items of its own toilet,
then flew off again, to a shadowy part of a crude wall
behind which someone was crouched, trying to hide.
Soon afterwards, it entered another house, landed,
and walked up and down for a little while on a table,
for reasons, one might say, not much known to itself.
Up and down it walked; then up and down again.
A bird will probably kill it in an hour or so
as a useful piece of food. Or so one might suppose.
But, for the moment, it walks about irregularly,
while three other beings elsewhere in the room
continue to do whatever it is they are doing.
And, by God, but it's something they ought not to be doing.

## Looking East from the David Hume Tower, Seventh Floor

For many months, off and on, I have glanced down from the window
in this high office, at all those other windows;
and the streets, and so much traffic, and the blue beyond.
And only now, perhaps exquisitely helped
by some unfathomable trick of the frosty sunlight,
have I ever seen anyone moving away over there
in one of those two, wide-faceted windows,
looking almost like enclosed balconies, above
an archway, just to the left of that obscuring
bulk of a nearby church which is evidently disused.
A couple of people are moving about inside the room, engaged
on some unintelligible task of domestic re-arrangement.
Or are there three of them? What are they quite doing?
And all those other windows still seem to be hiding nothing!

### 8

A casual glimpse through a curtain. Rain at night.
Doing what must be done for no particular reason.
I am not quite the person who should be watching it.

## Two Moments in the History of Planegg

### 1

A late walk. Already dark as I draw near home.
A kitchen window, lit, beyond a hedge.
Female arms working at a pot on a cooker.
Slowing a little, ambushed by so much warmth.

### 2

A week or so since I took this particular road.
A small house lying tight by a busy corner.
Yes! That bust of Mozart is still in the window.
But the profile is now turned a little further away.


## Planegger Holz

### 1

In the sunlit evening, I reach a roadside Pietà.
I take it seriously enough to stop for a long look.
Beyond the dark treetrunks, bright cars are driving by.
But they notice neither the breathing nor the wooden figures.

### 2

What's that? A wild, unreadable outburst of activity
at the front of a rough-hewn wayside Crucifixion!
A huge, unknown insect is caught in a spider's web.

*12.ix.01*

*Maria Eich*

Emerging from the trees behind the pilgrims' church,
then taking the way down towards the station underpass,
I could not at first make sense of the small group
I was approaching. But it soon resolved into
an elderly woman returning from a walk
with a small, youngish dog to a corner of the path
where an old man waited beside a rumpled, homely carpet
on which another dog sat. A huge presence;
ancient, almost incapable of movement.
It had been, clearly, a part of their lives for years,
but was only just still living. Without words, they began
a slow, laborious, clumsy trek to a nearby car;
their last outing together, or nearly their last.
Everyone silently wishing things were different.
Including a casual passer-by, heading down,
after a stroll that might have led him anywhere,
to his sister's flat, which they would never enter;
as they then drove back, likely enough to a flat of their own,
full, perhaps too full, of so much, such confused love.


# 12


So much to do to be here in this one specific foreign room!
Walk, underground, bus, aeroplane, train, train, walk.
But now a line of trees rustles in a secret lane below me.
While, back home, my clock must still tick on, an hour adrift.

## Looking for the Old Hunting Lodge

The last thing we expected to do was find a graveyard here.
But there they were. Row after neat row of foreign names.
Evidently some army had been caught in the wrong place.
You strolled off down one path. I sauntered off down another.
More traffic raced past as usual not far beyond the trees.

## A Trip to Starnberg

So: that Saturday morning we took the train to Starnberg
and the lake (the bright Starnbergersee – which is mentioned,
one knew, at the start of *The Waste Land*) where the mad king
(though I have never heard that phrase used here)
somehow contrived to drown. (And, as we approached it,
and looked out at the trees and streets and houses
which were almost insultingly real, I felt no great
sense of conviction that all these constituents
could be passed on, routinely, to the chaotic
workshops of memory.) Soon, after several streets
which were by no means quiet, we found a church garden
of immense, sheltered beauty. We inspected an ancient castle
which some malevolent being seemed to have transformed
into a local Tax Department of great and austere dignity.
(With the subtle hint of a dungeon for any reluctant payers.)
We admired the Alpine horizon. We watched a regatta
which happened to be taking place – inevitably, one felt.
A wonderful visit, in short. But there was also
at least one striking moment of more mundane pursuit;
when you deftly ducked through an alleyway and went into
a small supermarket – a local complexity
unfathomable to me. There you were sure you would find
a brand of tea impossible to lay hands on elsewhere.
You took two boxes down from a shelf, hesitated a moment,
then added a third to them. Better too many
than too few, I suppose. It's a fair old journey
merely to buy more tea. (In what bright kitchen,
I wonder, would that third box have been opened

had you not chosen it! I almost hear
the gay chatter of accompanying conversation.
And – oh, do smell these flowers!) But the fact remains,
when now I look back to that morning we spent there,
everything else is rather a background to those actions;
a glorious background, no doubt, but rather a background still.
Entering the daily life of the place was the real summit.
Yes. The peak of it all was the least exotic moment –
knowing that place existed, as it might be anywhere else,
knowing where the packets were to be found; deciding
to buy not one but two – no: not two but three.
Not three, but four. (No, wait a moment: not four.)


## 15

Is that a church-tower bell ringing in the next suburb?
I glance at my familiar watch. Yes; it quite possibly is.
My bag is packed, but I won't be leaving till tomorrow morning.
There's still time to go and look it out, if I want to.


### A June Evening in Scharoldstrasse

1

At six o'clock almost exactly
the thunder and lightning starts.

At times the sound of the downpour
drowns out the loud church bells.

Staying here on the deep balcony,
I move my chair for safety
a little further back.

I watch the sky for a long while,
with the street-map still in my hands.

2

By half past six,
the thunderstorm had ended –
though, since it was a Sunday,
the church bells rang on and on.

A bright, pleasant evening
was trying to slip into place
nonchalant, unseen and summery,

hoping that everyone important
had somehow failed to notice
it was turning up late for work

while a bright bird of a type
entirely unknown to me

but a common enough visitor
despite that, I suppose,

played about the garden
for a full two or three minutes
before flashing off out of sight.


## *Busy Tram, Löwenbrücke*

All these thousands of people
whom one talks to only once.
Yes. If even quite that.

A dry hurricane of uniqueness
through year after year.
Excuse me. And then gone.

Down the roads which only they know.
Or back behind the closed doors for ever.

So I gestured gently, to indicate
that she should take the last seat.

But she refused to take it.

## Würzburg

So here I am once again in the beautiful foreign city
and, yes, once again I am vaguely, uncomfortably aware
of how many beautiful foreign cities I am right now not in.

And I seem to be a denizen of the university district!
Ah, these students! These noble groups of youthful types –
so hopeful, looking to the future, and all that absolute nonsense.
Or all that comparative nonsense – I trust you know what I mean.

And how ghastly that my mind should fill with a sort of joyous abstract
    composition
of their neat little spare knickers lying about in light-filled rooms nearby
while the girls shout and laugh, as if youth happened only in this town –
which, on a morning like this, seems a not entirely unreasonable assumption.

God, yes, I am very sorry. Of course I wish the image had been
something much more expansive and heroic. But not to worry.
I intend to revisit some very famous monuments tomorrow.


## Bismarckstrasse

In my photograph of the beautiful old building:
someone's blue car parked across the road,
a woman in a yellow coat approaching the doorway,
a window wide open in the otherwise blank wall
of a neighbouring house. In that enchanting sunlight,
had what goes on in the heavens helped only a little
my shadow too might now have been visible
reaching up to that wall – but it is not.

## 20

I would like to bring that sunlight out of my dreams
and into this subtler world; which is, presumably,
somehow the source of that sunlight; placing it carefully –
carefully, carefully, and so carefully –
onto any suitable wall behind your head.
For what are walls for, but to frame your head;
or to keep the almost impossible in place, somehow;
as you talk about what you might do later this day –
things so important that they make language falter;
or my heart; or whatever the difficulty is;
when so much that was magic blossoms further into routine –
those who have slept inside the sun would half-guess what I mean –
here, not far away from (I suppose) a heedless star;
in a warm, untidy room, needlessly heated;
scented partly by happiness, partly by toast;
near a window from which I can see your parked car,
when I look for it; which, on some mornings, I don't.
For we may get used to anything, even staggering joy.
And talk as little as possible about what matters most.

### A Garnethill Bedsit

Ah God, the light that has fallen into this room
day after day! Where can it all have gone to?
Can a star do that? The kind and subtle starlight.
Shoes on the carpet. Oh yes, she bought the shoes,
but who bought the carpet? Some kind one who passed through
in a previous act of this endless, fateless improvisation.
So then. My thanks to all who made this possible –
early hydrogen, some exploding stars
and the bald chap who recently fixed that minor problem
with the hot water. Two decades ago – three decades –
much the same light came in through that window, I hope,
to worthy or pleased faces who knew the view
perhaps even better than we do now. Hello!
That dark wall there is the perfect height – isn't it?

## In Garnethill

More than once I have gone down this pleasant street,
this pleasant, slightly out-of-the-way street on the route
back from the station to the ground-floor room where I live
because of the memory of that dream-swathed Asian woman
who, in an absurd high box of a building, leant out
from an upper window in a wonderful early evening sunlight,
God knows why, as if looking for something legendary,
but perhaps only the arrival of an expected car.
She stood there in total silence. However, since I
was admiring a bright clutch of sunlit spires on the skyline,
my eye was caught by unexplainable colours nearby,
and I looked across and saw her, leaning as if to provide
a whole newly cleaned tenement building with an apt figurehead
before it sailed off enraptured into the pure, drenched, limitless light.

## Cutting on Impulse through Grant Street

All those lines of houses with masked lives going on within them!
What must we pass and miss, seeing only the blank walls.
All that resolute, unseen striding from room to room.
All that sitting in chairs, wondering what to do next.
A window swivels! A bow and dazzle of the wrong sunlight!

## In the Air

Strange, that I can still see
the front edge of the sunset
at its astronomical distance

but not the aeroplane wing
right there outside the window
where it is still pitch-dark

In my inside pocket, safe,
there's that photograph of you laughing –
though not at something I said


## 25

In this photograph of you, there is only you and the sky.
Which is to say, only you and something not really so important.
And a white bird wheeling through it, presumably ecstatic.


## Over a Dancing Bun

If you were falling through the sky, I would try to catch you, unquestionably.
But pretty much the reverse seems to be happening.
Does that make sense? Well, this new view from the window,
is, I must say, slightly disappointing. Insufficiently
like Claude, if you know what I mean. You know? French painter?
Unforgettable warm cloud effects; and, below them, a vision
of classical antiquity far too close to perfection
to be a convincing reconstruction. Though no doubt
we may love it for the construction it is in itself.

Oh, there is more to him than that – of course there is.
But surely every real thing has more to it
than the words we chase it with? This is hardly a weakness.
Or do we perhaps want a second universe to keep as a spare
beside the first? But then: to keep it where?
An academic question, if ever there was one!

## A More Cautious Icarus

That man up on the roof across the lane
behind your flat looks quite astonishingly tall!
I begin to have more respect for those old Greek myths.

Or might it perhaps be something in the atmosphere?
So close to a heaven of wonder and not knowing it.

Or perhaps he knows it. Perhaps that's why he's there.
No job at all. He just wishes to be near.

'Come down! Come down!' screams a possible nurse or policeman.
(A voice of civic responsibility from his childhood?)
'No! Absolutely not!' he replies. 'What is that music?
Something near here is near perfect, and I want to know what it is.'


## 28

A door closed on some floor above us as we were walking
down the stairway. One of the neighbours, no doubt.
If we had waited for merely a few more seconds,
we should have found out who, I suppose. But why wait?


## Queen's Crescent

We parked just round the corner from the house where I was born.
When did I last live there? Some thirty or so years ago.
You were extremely lucky, my darling, to find a place for your car.
It couldn't have been waiting empty even for a full minute.

## Under A Raized Sky

You parked in a lane; and when we came back to it,
over an hour later, after lunch in the restaurant –
a busy place, well-known to you, wholly novel to me –
somewhat to my astonishment, the car was still there, untouched.
Well, of course it was still there; yet somehow I was astonished
all the same. It had all seemed too rapturous
to convince daily life. More like half a lane, really.
Ahead of us, much sky and demolished walls.
What pale, fake past days were they once forced to make do with?
In their present destruction they had reached their perfect moment.
This will be a tricky manoeuvre, I think you said –
needing to struggle out in a skewed reverse,
the left wheels high, and a car not far behind you;
but you managed it with ease anyway. And I –
I wish you knew how ideally you drive your real car.
You seem to think it is not even an accomplishment.
An even trickier manoeuvre, I dare say,
if I may strain such grace to chase after significance,
as the one that the planet was performing, speeding
that small lane in its setting through so much space.
What if darkness is elsewhere? This is not elsewhere.
And those three or four other cars, already there,
whose choice we had so straitenedly to conform to;
whose unseen occupants no doubt soon enough
would have to attempt their own freeing manoeuvres –
even if for them (it is not impossible)
something should be here that they will never quite break free of.

## 31

Oh well, at least I should get to see a new restaurant.
But I find that when one enters the Underground system,
one is often caught unpleasantly between thinking of Eurydice
and wondering whether they've raised the ticket prices again.

The woman who was walking her dog on that football field
the last time I took the Edinburgh train
is no longer there. I hope nothing bad has happened to her.


## A Routine Tremor

I am walking along Great Western Road, doing my best
not to forget a deathless sentence, not quite daring
to nip into one of the public telephone kiosks
to note it safely down, and passing, as it happens,
the very street where a friend of mine lived some years ago
for a rather bizarre few months – when a newspaper placard
catches my attention, and whatever it was
I was carrying in my head is driven away for good.
Myra Hindley, it says, the much-discussed accessory
to a multiple child-murder, has just died in prison.
So: that becomes one way of having passed an existence.
I continue, as intended, into the charity shop on the corner
to look at the latest books they might have for sale –
but this time it seems there is nothing worthwhile to consider.


## At Sandyford Place

There was no other space left for me to use
between the cars parked by the kerb of the leafy road
and the wide pram pushed by (presumably) the mother
by the side of which the father (presumably) was walking.

But from just there a tree had at some point been removed,
and thus I was able to take a step up onto and over
the flat but slippery low remnant of its old trunk
and pass them without causing even a fleeting obstruction.

And I thought for a moment of what it must have been like
to look out from one of those windows above the adjacent railings
on so many autumn days, so many days of summer;

and see that phantom tree standing resplendently in view
the trunk of which I had so miraculously just stepped through
in an impossible morning, obstructed by living wood.


## Kelvin Way

Down there, in the part of the park which lies below
the cut-through public road which I am walking along,
wondering why I do not do this more often,
a father (I assume) is leading his small child
across the old, marbled bridge – where my own father
often used to bring me, almost half a century ago.
But what have such fresh things to do with half a century?
I watch a chance glimpse straining to become a memory.
I struggle to accept that this is not really me.
Another fine, bright winter day, so long after us;
so weirdly long after our many dozens of visits.
But this broad, leafy road, alas, only rarely
leads me directly enough to where I want to go next,
and now I have to leave it for another path,
go on up to an office in the University
and talk to various students (one by one by one)
in a high room with a window which must certainly
have lain within the range of both our visions
often enough back then, as we sortied over
that bridge ourselves. A high room, I suppose,
frequently occupied by other people talking,
whatever it was they were saying – something no doubt
well worth listening to, from time to time at least.

# Airalap: Second from the Left
## (i .e. An Impromptu, Revised As Little As Possible)

Looking out of this university attic, I sit and watch
the sun gorgeously setting behind the Sick Children's Hospital,
and suddenly remember that I was in there once myself,
at least four decades ago. What was all that about?
I had fallen off a tin drum – the room is not far from here,
as it happens – and, although the height was trivial,
it was enough to break my thin, boyish left arm.
(The only left arm I had at the time, I suspect.)
I can still vaguely remember the bafflement I felt
when my younger brother and sister, who were standing nearby,
sniggered as the men lifted me up onto a stretcher
and carted me, a ridiculous whimpering trophy, out of the flat.
The top floor – behind those two windows, up at the right.
Who the two men were I of course have no idea.
Nor even which parent it was whose anxious phonecall
brought them so briefly into my life, the latest
of the endless calls on their expert attention; many of them
no doubt fatal, even back then, in a world which seemed
mint-new, whatever else it was. So, off they bore me,
another atom of the traffic, to what in fact,
when I consider the point more closely, was surely *not*
the actual hospital I am looking out at now
from a dizzying position of mature social success –
the lines seem much too sharp and modern for that –
but instead an earlier building on much the same site.
Yes. Unless it's still down there, out of view, round the back somewhere.
Yes. Okay. Beyond the park, the traffic is thick, as usual.
The little river runs by much the same below the towers.
How long, I wonder, would I have to stand at this window
before I saw another ambulance? Not so long, I would guess.
After all, there's a larger hospital even nearer here.
I also remember the room I was sitting in when I turned thirty.
These days I talk to students who hadn't even been born by then.
None of them are here just now. Well, of course they aren't.
Thirty-five lines. Good God! And one more makes it thirty-six.
No, wait a moment. I've counted it wrong. *This* makes it thirty-six.
I'll probably visit that dark little restaurant later this evening.

Yes. I'm about due another visit. It must be a fortnight or so.
The owner's wife (is it?) has a wonderfully neat little backside.
Should I have said that? Yes, yes, yes: her small face
is exquisite too. One must be careful with the truth.
Besides which, the food there is genuinely good. Yes.
Really. The food there, I find, is usually very good indeed.
Of course, on some days it's better than others. Of course it is.
Well, for heaven's sake, how could that not be the case?


## Present

On what would have been
my father's latest birthday,

I go to check
that the house where I was born
is still there.

It is.


## Lines Written on My Father's Ninetieth Birthday

A warm stripe of late sunlight on the lawn you so often tended.
Can it already be almost a decade since you died?
For a moment, I find I am staring out at the garden,
jingling in my pocket keys for doors you never saw.

*20.06 22.vi.02*

## Making the Most of One's Chances

Another evening, and in a moment of sheer inadvertence –
that is doubtless what it was; what else could it have been? –
St Peter, closing up the gates of Paradise
for the night, no doubt more from habit than anything else,
finds, to his astonishment, that he has locked himself out.

A spasm of panic at first. He shouts for help.
(Whose attention, one wonders, is he trying to attract?)
He shouts again. No answer. He opens his mouth to shout
again – but this time, for some reason, he does not do so.
Instead he takes a look round. What is this place?

He takes another look round. What is this place?
It is so long since he had a good look round outside here.
He takes a few steps forward and back, looking round.
He stands motionless for a moment, thinking –
then shakes his head, laughs, and disappears down the road.


## The Evidence

### 1

A diver finds
a rotted human figure at
the bottom of the lake.

Eaten away to
nothing but skeleton
very many years ago.

And in the subtle hand-bones
so beautifully articulated
as if still clutched
is a small pilgrim's medal –

to guarantee safety
when crossing the troubled water,
the turbulent, troubled water,
the torrid, troubled, turbulent water

Or, as it turned out,
not to guarantee it.


2

But the thought was there anyway;
to make it seem as if
one had more control
than one truly had

And the rare medal is brought
into the local museum
after much administrative difficulty –

as an excellent specimen
an inspiring instance
of ancient local handiwork.

Which no doubt it is.

and also, I suppose,
as a sort of bonus,
an excellent specimen
of ancient local thought patterns

which can survive such setbacks
oh, at least as well

## Into the Same Lake Twice

So they dragged Peter with great difficulty back into the boat
and the Lord, who, by this time, was also on board
along with the others, sighed: 'O, ye of little faith.
We are extremely disappointed in you, Simon Peter.
Why didst thou doubt?' Whereat Peter, summoning up
the last of his self-control, replied: 'Doubt, Lord?
How can you lay that foul charge at my dripping feet?
I didn't doubt. There was never the slightest particle
of doubt in my mind. I sank; and that's the end of it.
Does all that floats have faith, and all that sinks lack it?
Does a spar of wood believe, and a stone not do so?
Does a boat lose its assurance when its floor is holed?
Would I have volunteered to follow your example
of walking on the water, if I had doubted you?
The accusation, Master, is self-evidently absurd.'

And the Lord said: 'Look, my son. Don't get me angry.
Don't twist my words. I'm ahead of you in that game.
The very fact that thou sankest showed that you doubted me.'

Whereto Simon Peter with calm integrity made answer:
'No, Lord. In truth, I trusted you implicitly.
I trusted you as I have always trusted you.
Every word. But the simple, brute fact is,
it can't be done. No. Anyone starting from here
and striding out onto the top of the water
will, in rather short order, begin to sink.
We neglect the simple facts at at our peril, Lord.
Such is, in sober truth, what the actual world is like.'

And the Lord said to Simon Peter: 'Very well.
You clearly require it to be proved to you again.
Watch me. I'll show you how it's done. Watch this.'

And he stepped over the side and disappeared.

# A Poem for the Final Year

So, they had gathered in the new conference centre
and it was going remarkably well, all things considered.
Problems about various holes in the atmosphere
and problems about various disappearing fishes
and problems about a wide range of matters in between
were all being broached. Perhaps they were not being solved –
perhaps, in the end, they would prove to be insoluble –
but they were at least being talked about in a way
more apt to lead to lasting, amicable answers
than other types of discourse looked likely to produce.
The local population was taking a certain interest;
it brought a fair bit of money into the city;
and correspondents and film crews from a wide swathe of countries
were reporting back on the difficult progress yet being made
with the aid of helpful pictures. Yes. It was that important.

Then, rather unexpectedly, there was a hellish loud crack.
A sort of moat formed round the edge of the building,
thickening by the second, with great lurching waves
suddenly spilling out of it; and the huge edifice
plummeted in accelerating turbulence
straight down through the slopping seas. A few people
managed to swim across, and were listened to
with real if short-lived interest, but most just disappeared.
There was a sudden lake where the vast building had been.

Various experts soon met at the site and agreed
it had all the hallmarks of something which simply couldn't happen.
And I dare say they were right. But tell me: what do *you* think?

# The Eternal Flame

At long last, his trial came on. After so much
speculation; after so much rage and alarm.
He said nothing. He chose to reserve his defence.
Whether we believe he had a defence or not,
he chose to reserve it, whatever it might have been.
He looked at the judge as if he was the judge.

The evidence was led, and it was utterly damning.
A building burned down, not only full of children,
but of maimed and crippled children; war-victims
who were there recuperating as best they might.
People broke down and sobbed, remembering the screams.
He looked at them weeping; his face gave nothing away.

'Did you think it was an act of mercy?' he was asked.
'Was it perhaps a miscalculation?' (He snorted.)
'Did you think it politically justified? Or morally?'
But he said nothing, except 'I am saying nothing.
Work it out for yourself as best you can.
You won't be able to, of course. But try your best.'

The judge did little but enumerate the facts.
He mentioned the wheelchairs, warped and twisted by heat.
He mentioned the smell of burning flesh. He mentioned
trapped hands poking through the bars. He mentioned the chain
of evidence, all of which led back to the figure in the dock.

The jury did not even bother to go into recess.
Hushed, harrowed and strained by what they had heard,
they pronounced him guilty by a unanimous vote.
There were cheers and lurid cries from the public gallery,
calling for something adequate to be done with the accused.
Screaming that he had done it, and why had he done it? Why?
An angry mob had massed outside, in an angry mood.
The police braced themselves. This would not be easy.
They were all assaulted, yet had to protect the assaulter.

'Have you anything to say why judgement should not be passed?'
the judge asked him. 'Well, actually, yes,'
he answered, and a bright light suddenly surrounded his head;
and he did one or two miracles with his manacles,
which brought gasps of astonishment from all round;
and he added with a delightful, self-deprecating smile,
'I have my reasons, and they are adequate reasons;
and not for you to judge. I am well beyond your range.
If you don't mind, I'll leave now. Work it out for yourselves.'

And half the court then stood up and burst into applause
and the singing of joyous, grateful hymns. And the crowd outside
cried out 'Hosanna!' and beat up an old atheist
who had muttered, 'Now, wait a minute. This can't be right.'
And the whole world was awash with gratitude and delight,
with the possible exception of the affected relatives –

and even a few of these were now trying out trusting smiles.
The defendant smiled back, waved, and became invisible again,
leaving only a tiny flame burning where he had recently been.


## The Mystery of Creation

The mural painter, putting the final touches
to an image of the Virgin and Child, high up
on the wall of a cathedral, took a sideways
step to observe it better, lost his balance,

and shaped to fall. However, the gracious Madonna
which he had just finished work on, reached out an arm
and drew him back to safety. A dazzling act
for all concerned. Or so it would have been

had the Child, presumably by accident,
not chosen that very moment to kick out furiously
with a young leg, catching the artist in the crotch
and sending him straight down to a sheer miraculous death.

## 45

Created a universe full of beings to praise Him?
Hmm. This chap must have very low self-esteem.
What he should have created was a decent psychiatrist.

## 46

I suppose one would prefer it if it were all just a little bit better.
On the other hand, how often does one actually read *King Lear*?
In the beginning, someone sat down and designed teeth. Is that right?

## *A Prodigy of Nature*

As the mighty herd of bison stampeded across the plain,
on one of those (to the outsider) unintelligible
impulses which seem to inspire them, resembling
a mindless panic as much as anything else;
one of the beasts near the back turned to his neighbour –
on the left – or was it the right? – and said to him:
'You know, my friend: this process begins to worry me.
I think I recognise broadly where we are.
The fact is, if I'm right, then very soon
we reach a cliff hereabouts; and, should we get there
at this speed, then we'll all be over the top
and dead, before we can even begin to slow down.
It's playing on my nerves, I don't mind telling you.'
To which the second, frowning, with sage demeanour replied:
'Look, mate. What do you or I know about these things?
We're not the leaders, are we? No. Strike a light!
Okay? Screw the bobbin! We are nowhere near the front.
It's for others to make those decisions, and for us
to follow them as responsibly as we can.
You this way, we this way too, if you take my drift.

Not abdicating our critical faculties –
no; I'm not saying that; certainly we must
retain our nerve and judgement – however, *au fond,*
we can't do it all ourselves, can we? No; we can't.
We have to trust the powers-that-be in a case like this.
We cannot decipher the whole world for ourselves.
Why would they call this a plain if it isn't flat?
It's sheer common sense. I'm not unsympathetic –
no, friend; I am by no means lacking sympathy
with your point of view – but events are moving so fast
we must go with them.' 'Right. Fair enough,' said his colleague,
as they disappeared in their turn head-first over the precipice.


## The Last Wave

Then came that terrible night when at last the rising sea,
driven by a combination of circumstances
which falls together perhaps once in a century,
reached the level and force required for it to
sweep over the dikes and the old barriers
which had beaten back for decade after decade
its previous outbursts, ravings and assaults,
knocking them aside along with the desperate new barriers
which were yet being hammered and flung up as reinforcement
even as the next surge suddenly heaved them aside –
and it sheeted vast tracts of land slowly won from it
over the previous centuries, at last able
to overwhelm an undefendable citadel
and claim back as much low-lying territory
as it could spread itself over in a single night –
more loss with each second; more drowning in each second;
a sense that this time all might be gone at once.
But even among the thousand local disasters
there were the occasional counter-moves; the occasional
successful defences; and there were many incidents
of success and failure mixed; of an uncertainty
as to which was which, and what might yet arrive.
Bells clanging; walls collapsing; boats everywhere –

winning and losing, commanded and uncommanded.
A world in waves, held by nothing, as if loose.
Some dead, some living, some disappeared, some screaming.
Thus it was that, for instance, in one place,
an island, as all worsened, the inhabitants
gathered together in the highest refuge there was,
a tight group crouched on top of the threatened sea-dike.
A preacher shouted prayers and voices shouted responses.
And a huge, climactic wave swept over them:
round the circumference of twenty or so men;
round the forty or so women and children within,
whom they were trying to shelter; swept right over them
and passed on into the further sea beyond,
leaving them drenched and buffeted, but unharmed.
And they, more or less kneeling, in response to this,
amazed, transported, began to raise their voices
in an ancient hymn of thanksgiving and praise.
Joyously, it floated out over the shattered land,
in scraps and patches blown this way and that;
until the great wave, rebuffed ahead and returning,
reached the now undermined foundation of the dike,
and wholly swept it away, along with all those who were on it.


## Beginning Again

After the, oh, innumerable stars and galaxies
had warped within their folds, or whatever it is they'll do,
and mere matter had so managed to contort or spread
as to disappear completely, taking with it
all the soldiers (toy and real), smeared particles,
back numbers of *Nature* – and, indeed, Nature itself –
into the great nothing which certain creeds
of perhaps excessive self-denial think is here already;

yes, after a couple or more of eternities had passed,
from somewhere within the void there came a modest cough,
and a voice, speaking a language which could hardly be specified,
started to marvel: 'Why? Oh, why? Why? Why?
Tell me: why is there nothing rather than something?
Why is there not not something? Eh? Who can tell me that?'

## A New Use for an Old Map

'With unforgiveable negligence, I farted'
(Pushkin, I think?) when she had left my room
for a mere moment. Instantaneous desperation!
At once I looked round for something – anything –
to fan the unworthy arrival swiftly away.
And the first thing to hand was my ancient, folding star atlas!
(Distinctly odd – since I had the clearest memory
of throwing it out last year. (I bought a newer one.
Which I rarely use either.)) Yes, yes – all right;
that should do it, I suppose. These minor breezes
among the stars! If everything else fails,
I can always pin the blame on astronomy. Yes.
And with some justice, surely. For, in the end,
it *is* to blame for all of this anyway, is it not?

## An Impromptu Apocalypse

Taking my ease within the West End Park,
I happened to let rip a tremendous fart
Which caused the birds to fall dead from the trees.
Nature grew silent. All the sky went dark.
Life vanished like a figment on the breeze.
And the Cosmos did the opposite of start.

# Various Casual Assemblages

Another charming afforested walk through the suburbs;
and, at one point, another charming woody graveyard!
A few hundred more lives which are over, waiting patiently
for no-one. There may be visitors who stumble upon them;
there may be visitors who deliberately arrive,
clutching mementoes, with fading days and nights
flickering in their heads like fatally injured songbirds.
There may well be no-one there for hour after hour.

Or possibly we stroll through, scarcely pausing in our talk.

For, in truth, we have many important things to talk about.
We nearly always do, don't we? Let's see. What next?

Isn't it charming how we can all kick the bucket?

Or perhaps I should dig up another word than 'charming'.
And possibly another phrase than 'dig up'.
And certainly another term than 'bucket'.

Yet the whole planet is that sort of place already, isn't it?
You know: the remnant of numberless and unremembered graveyards.
Despite our occasional tending of favoured corners,
it gets a bit more like that the whole time, in fact.

This sort of worrying scrap floating through outer space!

Is it really the right place for quite that kind of thing?

And suburban graveyards speeding *en masse* through the sky?
At times it can all seem so chillingly devoid of dignity.

But then we went round a couple of quiet corners,
and chanced upon a wonderful open-air restaurant.

How I wish we could have stayed there for even longer than we did!

# *Annaniana*

## 1

Since it was human beings after all
Who invented photography, we naturally think
We human beings should be able to deal with it.
But look there! A human being leans against a bridge,

Ignoring the crowds all round, resting his hand
Pensively at his chin, while, beside him,
A young boy rests on his elbows. A carter
Is looking over at them as he passes by to wherever.

## 2

One photograph of a crowd crowds out our history books;
One nonchalant sunlit moment will involve more
Than anything our largest computers can store.
And, even so, most things are nowhere recorded.

They have all crossed that bridge and disappeared.
And I who have afterwards crossed that same bridge often
Thought not for a moment of them, and for scarcely a moment
Of those who might be crossing the bridge along with me.

## 3

All right. A colossal crowd is crossing a bridge.
An overwhelming number of ancestral horses
Cast lightning shadows on a now forgotten day
Of the last century. When are people not passing?

My glance could settle on any one of them;
Could still settle on any one and be hugely defeated –
In this large cool carpeted room in a library,
Where I sit right beside a woman in a pink summer dress.

4

Picking its way through a bridgeful of horse-drawn traffic,
Between two rivers of people, all wearing
Elaborate, complex clothing as naturally
As the sun picks out their shadows in the old photograph,

Goes the open-top horse-drawn public carriage, bearing
Its still visible load of men, most of them
Hunched slightly forward in thoughtful silences,
Permanently not quite speaking to each other.


## The Historic Inner City

1

The sun rises again on the small leafy cemetery
over the wall from the office parking-spaces,
and another day's light picks out the old inscriptions.

*He was disliked by someone powerful.*
*He almost invented a new religion.*
*He thought he was the centre of the universe.*


2

At lunchtime, in the warmer weather, some secretaries
dot the low walls and the grass, eating sandwiches
and asking each other what they should do about him next.

*He believed he was in touch with at least one other world.*
*He was killed by a stone hand which fell from a roof.*
*He committed a terrible crime and was never found out.*

3

Yet at evening this part of town is almost deserted.
Occasionally someone might wander through to a nearby flat,
I suppose; where somebody else is possibly waiting.

*He talked to no-one, and yet he was very happy.*
*He talked to everyone he met and looked fairly content.*
*He seems to have left lately, but nobody noticed him go.*


## A Reasonably Long Run

Keynes died a few days short of his sixty-third birthday –
hardly old, but not a strikingly premature death either.
Yet both of his own parents were able to attend his funeral.

As if the universe really were moving backwards.
The world ends – and one is somehow left in existence.
Yet another hour still free for amusement before bedtime.

His wife, the Russian dancer Lopokova,
said she missed him so much that, for some years afterwards,
she wore his old pyjamas, trying to keep him near her.

*Da.* A heart-warming tale, if it had ended there.
No more, for sure, than so great a man deserved.
But, alas, it seems that that was not where it ended.

For, not many years later, she remarked wonderingly:
'When he died, I suffered a lot. I thought that I could *never*
live without him. Yet now I never think of him.'

'Never' was the word she used, I believe. Oh, yes;
a great man, no doubt; but death can be so endless.
And there comes a time when one simply has to change one's pyjamas.

Morning. Unsettled light. White pyjama trousers
lying beside the front door, with a newly arrived letter
on top of them. It must surely be good news this time.


## Background Music

Another morning
with the clink
of our spoons
and cereal bowls.

Time to tear off
the latest page
from the astronomical calendar
on the kitchen wall

Ah yes! One more
massively exploding galaxy,
somewhere or other.
Very nice. So.
Tea or coffee, my
darling?

## Excelsior

The first day of the year yet again. Yet again,
a sense that now is the moment for astronomy
to perform some quite astonishing sky-burst of a feat.
But, yet again, it doesn't; and one is left
(thank God) to put up another new calendar
just where its ruthlessly discarded predecessor
was sited, between the wall-tiles and the door.
And so it happens that, trying to rub off
what looks to me like a dust smudge in a top corner
of a colourful view out over the Karwendel Alps,
I find I am not succeeding. Strange. I look again.
Aha! That might explain it. Let us start the year
as we mean to go on: in pursuit of the highest tasks!
I am trying to brush away a fading crescent moon.


## 59

In the second week of February, at last
I remember to turn over the calendar in my office.
Hmm. Yes. An impressive sunset. Still, I think
I preferred January's picture – whatever exactly it was.


## 60

I admit I am impressed by the arrogance of the sun:
that permanent, far-off explosion which yet dares
to try to alter the pattern on your walls;
thereby aiming to claim some colleagueship in the universe
with a piece of lined paper beside a calendar
on which you have scribbled a phone number. Just a moment.
I hope you don't mind me asking – but whose is that phone number?

## 61

Onto the last page of the calendar yet again.
There are always more views to be seen among these mountains.
Neither the prettiest picture, nor quite the ugliest one.
Another irreplaceable scatter of lights behind the windows.


## An Immensely Rare Sort of Moment

At last the final morning of the 1900s!
We knew they would have to end; but how disconcerting
to be so unable to make the slightest difference.
Seagulls circle with a familiar nonchalance
rather nearer the neighbouring slate roofs
than to the grey-white sky. Through a side-window
I watch a woman in a lavender anorak
walk down the street. She passes, and disappears.
Next, a red car. And, at a neighbouring window
across the road, to the right, a slight figure
dressed in purple stands for a few moments,
does something, and goes away. She too is wholly unknown to me.
The clock shows yet another unemphatic quarter to ten.
Again, there is nothing particular needing to be said.


## Next Day

The door quickly opens, and –
yes! There she is again!

I step in. Yes! That
is exactly the same new carpet.

She begins to talk. And yes!
That is surely the same voice!

Yes. Or almost the same voice.
Certainly close enough for the moment.

Perhaps my over-burdened memory
simply couldn't quite hold it.

Yes. So. Only one question left to ask.
But, my God – what a question!


## 64

Through the door I can see another door.
A voice reaches me haphazardly through a pair of doors.
Talking to the cat, I suppose. What else could it be?


## 65

At the very moment when I thought you might telephone me,
I was in fact phoned up – by another woman!
Hmm. This telepathy business just needs a *little* more work.


### A Return Ticket

In two minutes' time, the train
should leave this coastal station.

A distant, wrought-iron bench
stands right beside the sea.

But no-one is sitting on it.
Particularly not you.

No. You are elsewhere entirely.

And note, at the water's edge,
that pair of matching telephone kiosks.

One should have been enough.


## How It Seemed to a Late Contemporary

I stand, waiting, in the station. The train is ten minutes late.
From here I can see a line of some half a dozen phone booths.
Only one of them is occupied at this particular moment.


### 68

I can picture exactly the well-lit and loved room
where you must be as you answer my call on the telephone.
But you have no idea yet where I am talking to you from.
I could still be away on the other side of the country –
or round the very next corner. (Where I in fact am.)


### 69

Looking after the house for a friend – (they are in Portugal) –
I take a call from a friend of *his* in Japan.
A daughter was born to them two days ago! Great
news! I hurry back to a cooling, half-finished meal.


### 70

The orange I picked up a week ago in Inverness
I at last unpeel and eat in a fine room in Glasgow.
The strange thing is, this isn't even my house.

## 71

Night. I sit in Dundee eating raisins I bought in Glasgow.
Part of the yearly produce of California, evidently.
My sister left here on Monday, to go to work in Germany!

## 72

Night. Throughout the city, they are
discussing the future, no doubt; while I nip down
to the parked car, to fetch up some fizzy drinks
which you forgot to bring up with the rest of the
day's stuff. So many parked cars! So much traffic! So
much! And so many babies no doubt tossing
and turning in something not quite like real sleep
hereabouts, as I hurry back up the stairway.

## Not on the Schedule

In the shade of the ancient building, hurriedly
we shared out a snack, with a vague sense of disturbing something
which ought to be left alone. The harsh past, presumably.

'Yes! Leave us alone!' the ghostly voices whimpered.
'This place is closed. We thought we were significant!
We schemed. We skirmished. We maimed each other and so forth.

Just finish the ham sandwiches and get out of here at once!
How can you possibly drink that fizzy rubbish anyway?
It isn't right. How dare you take up so much space? Go! Go!'

'Are you happy here?' she asked. 'Yes,' I said. 'Yes.'
'That's good,' she went on. 'Did you bring a map?' 'A map?
No.' 'Oh well then,' she said; 'in that case, I won't even ask.'

## The Canals of Mars

Think of any one day
in, say,
the whole nineteenth century.

All that movement
at points of the earth.
And for what?

A bluish planet.
A dot in the sky.
Not much.

What of all that remains?
Not much.
Not very much.

You left a glove here
on your last visit,
by the way.


## In the Shadows

The last lights
across the street
go out eventually.

You left me with much
to think about
before you went off to sleep.

Life is good, yes.
I won't try to deny it.

However, extinction
should be quite nice too.

## Advice From the Wall

You see that photographed
dot in the distance?
Yes. That is me. Quite possibly.
Isn't it?

No.
Not the one beside it.
Not north, south, east or west.

All right?
Any complaints to make?
None?
All right then. Listen.

Just close the ageing book;
forget its wavy images;
clear away a few plates,
and, if she's still here
here or hereabouts
tell her again you love her.

Always assuming
that you do love her.

Perhaps you don't?

In that case,
don't.

In that case, just clear out.

## A Run of Surfaces

After some difficulty in falling asleep,
largely through thinking of my mother, who is surely
dying of cancer in a nearby different town
from this one, where she spent so much of her life;
I dream, for the first time in many years,
of her own mother. How I was visiting her
in the house with which we always associate her –
or *I* do, at least, since she was living there
when suddenly she appeared as an aspect of my life:
another place to go to; another person to visit;
somewhere else where I was surprisingly
known and talked about. Up that staircase again,
after an interval of three real decades,
that real staircase still a brief walk from here;
to her door, while an overwhelming gold light
blew through a window at the top of the stairwell –
A real window? An imaginary window?
Is it something the light can truly do in those windows?
I have no idea. It seemed we were closer than ever.
Astonishingly close. But then some classical music
awakened me, a brief pianistic run
from the flat right above; a recording of some sort,
from what I suppose is a young boy's room. It is so curious.
The morning, I suppose, is only a moderately bright one.
I have never heard classical music come from that room before.

## 78

Walking home from the train station on a rainy, unsure night,
because I had forgotten to bring my underground ticket with me
and didn't want to pay for my mistake,
I found that I, without directly planning it,
was about to pass the tenement where I had spent
the first sixteen years of my life. The rain was heavy now,
and I suddenly thought to go through the outside door again
and investigate a place which had once been so familiar to me.
But, on the first landing, I heard a noise somewhere above
of young voices laughing and talking with each other;
and I thought to myself: it would be better to leave
rather than have to encounter them. Which I did –
passing at the foot of the stairway an old side-door
which I do not at all remember ever having seen before.


### West Princes Street

Walking again down the street past the flat where I was born,
I glance up, as I nearly always do on such occasions
at the five-beat line of large windows beneath a roof
which are clearly the most crucial part of the whole building.
(Odd that all the others should *still* be quite so secondary.)
One of them is slightly open – a mild surprise
in such cold weather. Who has had the impudence
to leave ajar, without the least consultation,
a window I knew so well how to live behind?
Near which I had so many hopes and tantrums.
Which I looked out of God knows how many thousand times –
and saw how many now vanished people passing by,
most of them needless, old, preoccupied strangers;
who have now so strangely become an unsure passer-by myself.

## Whatever It Was

Walking to a friend's house on a dark chilly evening
not long after the clocks have been once again
dislodged back an hour, I happen to revisit,
for a couple of blocks, the street where I was born.
Beyond the building where, I think, ballet dancers now train –
in those earlier years, some sort of army depot –
(*plus ça change*) – a black shape takes up a threatening pose
in the centre of the pavement. Hmm. What could that possibly be?
A box? Perhaps a fridge? An abandoned safe? No. No:
at close range it resolves into an ordinary cooker.
(The design is clearly old-fashioned but not yet rare.)
Ah, all that past warmth and happiness, or whatever it was,
dispersed to nothing visible in this old, cold street –
with no more company than those few bright windows nearby!


## 81

Over thirty years after finally leaving this building
in which I was brought up, I pass its street-stairs again
on my way to the train station. Nearby on the pavement –
more domestic rubbish evidently waiting to be picked up –
are an old record player and an ironing-board.
Ah, all those wrinkles smoothed! All that music listened to!
Quick! Quick! There is still time! Let me listen to
the other side of the record, while I iron this shirt –
perhaps before putting it on and walking to the station
through streets knocked down below the vast new motorway
which tore up those old lives. And as I sit on the train
taking me through to Edinburgh yet again,
I will try to remember them in all the fine detail
that once I knew so well, and I shall of course fail.

## The Road Not Not Not Not Not Not Not Taken

I am moved by the perfection of the sights
one sees through swiftly passing windows. For instance,
those impossibly neat, clean occupiable kitchens
containing flat objects of a dazzling whiteness,
or flowers, it appears, eternal, perfectly chosen,
which must be adding scents to immensely alive lives.
A couple caught in a mutual warm embrace
in a fleeting suburb of some negligible town
which one passes through, intending never to visit;
turning one's head this way, or just as well that way,
till the train stops on its present most significant occasion
and one sets off on the next stage of one's own journey
towards a loved room, or an as yet quite unknown one.
Or up one of these stairways – yes, quick: up one of these stairways!


## A Couple of Measured Paces

*for E.M.*


1

Years later, I learned that Gerard Manley Hopkins
had worked in Glasgow – and in St Joseph's Church! –
which I too (though it wasn't our normal place of worship)
visited a few times in my youth. Now all those roads
have been devastated, including the shop at the corner
which housed my father's opening independent venture
as a small electronics trader. Oh, I remember it well;
particularly the huge, treacherously floored cellar,
where I scouted about for hours among so much debris
of the previous owner – (a printer?) – while waiting for my father
to finish his afternoon's work and drive me home after school.
That vault was surely in place already, a century before,
as Hopkins worked for a few months in an uninspiring district,
unknowingly passing, perhaps, cellar after occupied cellar.

2

I think I learned that fact about Gerard Manley Hopkins
from a sonnet by Edwin Morgan. I certainly remember
in one of the outer, lesser Glasgow University buildings
being told by him directly (apropos a book of mine
which dwelt at some length on the streets and doors and windows
of my now misplaced childhood) that an aunt of his had lived
just across the street from our top-floor flat, and clearly
visible from up there. I too must surely have seen her,
doubtless more than once, in all those overlapping years.
Indeed, since often he used to go and visit her there,
I very likely also saw the poet himself. People
came and went, and one did not think to ask why.
What did it matter? A few more children run by
a man who has not quite reached his aunt's door yet again.


## Poem Found Scribbled at the Back of an Old Book

My occiput (a label which I learned only yesterday)
rests awkwardly against the headboard of my bed.
I have not yet drawn the white cord just above me, which
will put out the light for the night. The onset
of sleep has disappeared into the sound of a clock
very slowly striking midnight in the back-room below
(an old manual model, clearly in need of winding up)
and the taste of the sharp pencil lying against my lips.
My parents are in a room underneath, perhaps sleeping –
both; or only one of them; or neither of them.
My brother perhaps is asleep in another room underneath.
(And as I write the word 'brother' awkwardly, with the pencil,
I hear the sound of a door quietly opening downstairs.)

*00.13 7.x.87*

## On a Brief Visit

Looking through an old paperback, I unearth
these three lines jotted down inside the end cover
and dated, to almost exactly six years before:

*The same window she looked out of so many times.*
*Between two and three years now after my mother's death.*
*Two men are building a wall in a neighbour's garden.*

I have not the least recollection of writing them.

But, since I can still do so, I go across to the room
where my mother lived through most of her final months.

Again, the road beyond is active enough to reward
whoever wants to observe it, for whatever reason.

And the wall too must still be there, I suppose,
though I am not at all certain what wall it was.

By now it has long since blended completely into the view.


## Actually, It Didn't

Clearing out the back of an unkempt bedside drawer
before I move elsewhere, I discover among the debris
the small battery-driven fan my mother often used
in the warm days of her last summer a decade or so ago.

After her death, I had brought it here with me,
a treasure beyond the expression, associated forever
with those raised, precious months not quite in normal time.

I placed it with great care in this drawer beside my bed –
and, soon, while life went on with its one damn thing
after another, I – dear God! – forgot about it completely.

Gently, I press the switch. Our daily routine
walks hand in hand with oblivion. I press the switch –
but nothing moves. I press the switch again.
It stutters for a moment, before whirring into life.


## 87

Blustery showers. Children are hurrying to school through them.
There is still so much future up there, just ahead, after all.
Actually, not a few of them are walking with striking slowness.
Perhaps they think pneumonia is their more attractive option.
Two years to the day since my mother died; having seen this view so often –
a sleepless witness, here, of the events of dawn, and later;
from this very chair, looking over that still grey gate,
to the quiet road that leads down to the flower-shop.
To others too, of course; but, firstly, to the flower-shop.
I shall be visiting there myself, in an hour or so.
I put my breakfast plate down onto the broad, wooden window-ledge.
A white car, registration number F 429 Something,
hurriedly passes this house too, for some reason or other.


## 88

I sit near an open window, reading a play by Pinero.
Suddenly I hear my mother's voice in the nearby garden –
talking to a passing neighbour. I had not known she was there.
I expect she knows I'm here. (Where else would I be?)

## 89

Wakening up from an unintended afternoon nap in a chair,
I eagerly glance to my left. No glowing table is waiting there.
Ha! I *knew* the price was simply too good to be true.


## A Prayer, Particularly Superfluous

I had such a vivid dream that you were alive.
I wrote it down at once. And now, to my grief,
I find I cannot even remember where I wrote it down.

Merely losing the reality was not enough
for your idiot son. No. He had to lose the dream too.

Forgive me. You know how I was always losing things.


## A Cosmic Footnote

Alas, a copyist has introduced a few errors
into this classic text about the unity of opposites;
making it seem to mean something else entirely.

## The Greatest Poem in the World

Well, that was all very interesting. And all so curiously life-like.
I dreamt I had created the greatest poem in the world.
Somebody has to do it, I suppose.
There was a sort of ceremony going on to acknowledge the fact.
The architecture was stunning, and the praise, it seemed, sincere.
Oh, dear. I am truly sorry I woke up quite so soon.
I was fair basking in the endless warmth and admiration.
Someone even quoted to me a passage from it. Two lines.
I wrote it down eagerly as soon as I woke up,
lest I forget. What a loss that would have been.
The greatest poem in the world, and quite forgotten.
Not that that won't be happening in the fullness of time anyway.
So, it turns out I did write some of it after all, even though
what went fore and aft of it is apparently lost for ever.
And yet, not all is lost. There remains this orphaned couplet:
*Any star that is visible is too bright –*
*even though your knees are visible in the daytime.*
The strange thing is, I know exactly what he meant.

## Four Mistranslated Sonnets

### 1  Hillhead

Snow is falling onto the travel agent's
and onto the pub beside it. All those places
that I have never been to, listed in the window
at temptingly keen prices! No use. No use.
They cost too much anyway, but that isn't really the point.
I would like to see the Greek islands, but not right now
when a stranger and deeper destination entices me.
I am going to a flat right at the top of this hill!
Three connected rooms. Three! Space enough
for the richest life. This slope which I have dealt with
hundreds of times in years gone by, without
for a moment suspecting its capacity for joy,
I now inspect with awe like a recent visitor to this planet.
For now I must start to make sense of tangled legends of my own.

### 2

Merely sitting in the same room, talking to you,
I am thinking, 'This is it! This is it at last!'
Let the clock and the calendar do whatever they like.
Let the sudden workmen on the road outside
do whatever it is they think they are doing
in preparation for something or other in the future –
some facility improved; some thoroughfare made better.
Something, they think, not pointing straight at today.
This is it, the thing itself, even as it is.
It will never wear anything greater than that striped top of yours.
You know, I simply cannot believe that mere machines put your clothes
    together.
I mean if they can do that, why can't they make everyone happy?
It should be a simple matter of changing a couple of switches.
And I speak here, note this well, as a fully trained electronics engineer.

3

Since now the sunlight of this late July afternoon
has come so far as to reach the vase on the window-sill
against which I had earlier propped up a photograph
of your face laughing in sunlight several months ago –
for on the star saunters, sustaining years and spaces,
whether you have been able to come here with me or not –
I bring the image down, onto the shadowed table-top,
suddenly worried that my negligence
might be causing it to fade. Oh, everything will fade,
no doubt including the sun, but for my worsening eyesight
to outlast this shining paper would be too great an embitterment.
Outside, there is a large garden in which someone else is sunbathing –
and beyond it almost the most beautiful lane I have ever seen.
Even so, it can stay unoccupied for hours at a time.


4

For the two weeks I was there, I never saw my neighbours;
but then, on the final afternoon of my stay,
I was sitting reading silently on the downstairs balcony,
when, beyond the partition wall, from the balcony next door,
two slim forearms started to shake out a green jacket,
dispersing dust, or whatever it was, over the shared, sheltered back lawn.
Obviously someone who assumed she was alone.
Someone of whom I never saw any more than those arms.
All that past, all that (as I suppose) future
unknown to me. I sat for a minute or so,
ignoring my rather stupid book on the Turin Shroud (really –
which I later threw into another unknown neighbour's rubbish bin),
admiring the elegant unknown hands at work for a few moments,
before they disappeared back into whatever life contained them.

5

Even in that one smallish city I saw three or four places
where I had to live. Places which not to live there
meant one's life had to be – I'm very sorry – a failure.
But the perfect sites are doubtless blocked up by one family –
perhaps by a single old wasp who has simply forgotten to die –
for decades at a time. Oh! Not to look out
of one's kitchen window, and see across the back lane
that soaring dome – or not to be able to leave
that presumably large front room and go out onto a balcony
like an open theatre box, looking across to a park
in the shelter of the overhanging upstairs windows!
Not to have that small square outside, always there to be gazed at!
Kindly direct me at once to the manager's private office.
It is all so loosely arranged. Which of these doors is it?


## A Question of Order

A short, falling sidestreet, with a park at the bottom of it.
Down there, a tenement turret looks out onto high trees.
A woman is standing thoughtfully at the top-floor window.
A huge plant stands in the same window of the floor just below.


## 95

Still fairly dark this morning. I stand near the window –
not yet quite back inside the challenging role of myself.
In the building across the lane, a light suddenly goes out.
Well, well. At least one person is already making decisions.

## A Partick Morning

What? Can thousands of the world's streets
contain feelings very like this?

And yet, I suppose they must.
Yes. Yes; of course they do.

But why is there never anyone
in those darker rooms
across the road?
One never sees anyone there.

Slowly the sunlight moves across
so many other people's belongings.


## Over There

Flicking through TV channels
in a Copenhagen hotel room,

directly across the road
from a fascinating corner

where in an upper window
a beautiful white vase stands
like a notice board for Paradise

and where often at night
a subdued golden light seeps out
from a highly discreet nirvana

I find myself looking
at pictures sent from the surface
of Mars a few years ago

and am impressed by how greatly
it looks like anywhere else.

Though not quite everywhere else.

No. That would be to claim
just a little too much for it.

## Byres Road

I leave the flat in the morning
and walk down the stairs to the
strange sudden brightness of the street.

None of it in the slightest
possible without oxygen.

The moon so high and faint –
pretending it's an illusion.

Imitating an illusion;
pretending it's not here.

And now I seem to remember
the moon requires no oxygen.

But that's a mere detail
and my bus is due along soon.


## The Same Raver

All right. Another morning.
Another crust to be earned.
The same train journey
to Edinburgh yet again.

However, something seems
unfathomably right with
every second or third view
on this particular day.

Did I dream well last night?
Was my breakfast perhaps
drugged into euphoria
by some unseen visitor?

for on such mornings
we see the doors closed
by unseen friends
just ahead of us

Look there, for instance!
That familiar old tenement,
standing high above the bank
behind yet another bridge.

I have never been sure
where it shows up on our maps
for the level earth seems
to rob it of its stature

No. Where is it and why
does it look quite so hopeful?
It has turned at once into
its own site of legend.

Who is speaking there
under some enchantment
while an unseen train
slithers past nearby

and who is there listening
to those scarcely credible words
or to a magical silence
caught between two worlds

as the dead wall sings

the dead walls come alive
our mere strings of air
give orders to the stars

## A Sonnet in the Wrong Language

Sunlight. Late for work and running to the car.
Not me – her. I watch through a gap in the curtains.
That street was surely never fully here before this morning –
despite those fluked old photographs of a place with the same name.

Oh, if only the entire universe had a wife to love!
(Or a husband – that detail is not particularly important.)
I do not even insist on the technicalities of matrimony.
After all, one expects the whole world should be somewhat hard to match.

But it too could look out the window, and see her drive off to work.
And think: what are my streets that so much should happen in them?
A wild glimpse through a gap in the calm halves of a curtain.

Wasn't there something else about a curtain? Ah, yes.
The immense, angry crowd shouts for a long time, then vanishes.
Later, enough light pierces the curtain to show a sleeping face.


## A Border Ballad: The Fantasy of the Invisible Friend

Help me, dear! The atoms are dressing in old clothes,
the tired flirts, evidently so convinced of our own
gullibility in all actual things, that they
think any trivial subterfuge will confuse them.

We have seen those shapes before! We have seen those
shapes before! – we shout at them, forgetting
that our eyes are only ours for a short loan.
Weeds are waiting patiently for their own turn to use them.

### Chorus

No. Actually, I have only once ever made a phonecall
from an apparatus in the town where she was born.
Curiously enough, I made it to my own mother.
*And* I can pretty well remember all I said to her.

Thus pupils turn the corner, and thus planets
fall sideways through more space for a few billion
brilliant academic careers. Will we be heard of,
the fresh lakes whisper anxiously to each other

as they dry up in a manner which seems swift
to them. To whom? To them. No, you shall never
be heard of, chorus those quiet birds that sheer towards
their lineal descendants; those who at an

*Chorus*

Hee hee hee hee hee. Was your mother a pederast?
Most unlikely. The stags are exploding extremely late this year.
Can it possibly be, do you think, that they've missed the bus?
*(What bus? I don't know. Maybe the two that just passed.)*
Remember that time we saw an angel at Luss?
Or was that someone else? Yus; quite possibly it was.

impossibly inconsiderate hour of the morning
insert their jabbing calls into the eardrums
of all the sleepers lying barely a wall away
from this vindictive garden. One of them

is, of course, woken – I am almost always wakened
at such an hour. Another nearly wakes;
but the unshared heart is given a shared shuddering.
Another rises in her sleep, and walks past –

*Chorus*

O time! O teeth! O eyes! O death! O heart!
Sometimes we talk of Descartes. Sometimes we fart.
*(Sometimes we are able to do both at almost the same time.)*
Have I no future left? I am not complaining.
For on her too, at this moment, the same sky must be raining.
Bong!

Shut up. I have no idea what she walks past, or whom.
Neither have you. And neither, now, has she.
Anyway: if she knew that, she would not be sleeping.
And, if she is not sleeping, then what else might that room –

*Final Chorus*

Prince, there can be no ultimate conflict between the black pieces of good
and the white pieces of evil, nor between Heaven and Hell.
For the Lord is himself playing both sides of the board at once –
even when he gets someone else to move the men for him.

Sometimes it is too difficult for us; sometimes it is far too simple.
And, by the way, how far is it from Duns Scotus to Dalrymple?

## On His Obscure Hort

When I consider that I may have lost the call to strangle a bangle
while still on the pricking cusp of my intellectual prime,
then, frankly, I run around saying unspeakable things about Time,
or singing the song which late the Sirens sang all.

Then feel I like an ancient broken bowl – severely over-blimming-priced –
which, rattling like a knack on a shelf a thousand and one years,
at length tips over, sweet soul, clear into the abyss,
and falleth on a sleeping head, which cries out, 'This! Filth!'

(Or perhaps, 'Piss!') Oh, sparkling (w)rack! How close to thee
cometh the careworn, mourning, lifetorn, cavewoman heroine,
who, seeing all, my captain, or seeming all to see –
like as the rampant corpse upon the darkling cliff,
desiring these three darling waves to curve within
this daring cavern, declaims: No worse a curse than if

## An Ode Suitable for Almost Any Literary Occasion

Yes! To be the flea that bit Shakespeare! Yes!
To be one of the little bastards that lived off Shakespeare's blood!
That must have been quite a life, surely? Yes! The great Willie!
Actually, there were probably a good few dozen of them in all.
Hundreds, perhaps. Of fleas. Maybe even thousands.
I don't know. What were conditions exactly like back then?
I don't know what conditions were exactly like back then.
I have not the least idea of his standards of personal hygiene.
Go on! Bite the bastard! Yes! Bite the bastard again!
(Odd, is it not, how even in high artistic matters
private questions of animosity will keep on breaking in,
won't they?) Yes! Bite! Look! Look at him scratching
his neck, or feet, or behind; or even, for that matter, his willie –
unless perhaps that's merely a discreet bout
of self-abuse, as he works away at his latest piece
of sublime poly-expanded transcendental plagiarism!
Or on writing yet another of his appalling poofy sonnets.
Yes! Bite! Go on! Give him no peace! He deserves none.
Quite apart from the truly atrocious handwriting.
And dead at fifty-two – that wasn't too great, was it?
I mean, even Ben effing Jonson managed to beat that out of sight.
And dead on your birthday to boot! Huh. Happy birthday,
Bill. Many happy returns and so on
and so forth. An extremely special day for literature,
obviously. All that work, and thousands of halfwits –
maybe millions of them – broadcast over the globe
(Sigmund bloody Freud, to give but one example)
think someone else wrote the plays! Somebody. Anybody.
Anybody but you. They don't even think you did it!
Ha ha ha ha ha ha ha ha ha.
Or they don't think you did some of it because the writing's so *bad*!
Dear me. No glory lives behind the back of such? Eh?
And we all know Tolstoy's thoughtful opinion of *King Lear*.
Well, I will say this for fleas: at least they're free of value judgements.
Though no doubt they prefer some types of blood to others.
Who wouldn't? So. On you go then. Bite! Yes! Bite! Bite!

# Fate

I almost called this poem, *The Literary Life*.
Right. A was a man of very great verbal gifts
who thought that much could be explained by astrology.
(For even great verbal gifts, one finds more and more,
are no guarantee that the other things are there too.)
He met B at some drunken literary party –
she bit his face, and he thought 'This is the one!' –
whereas C met D on a ship on the broad Atlantic.
Some time later A and B, married, sublet a flat
to another couple, but then met C and D.
They liked them greatly, tore up the first cheque,
and rented the place out to the latecomers instead.
Soon afterwards, A and D had a passionate affair,
then B killed herself. Not long after that,
D, the second woman, also killed herself;
and killed E too along with her.


# Two Japanese Temple Scenes

1

How wonderfully calm the temple garden is this evening!
The lawn and the fallen leaves lie warm in the late sunlight.
Wisdom seems almost to have taken on living form.
Even that small pipe sticking up through the turf
Does little or nothing to compromise the peacefulness.
If one observed it at all, one would presumably think it
Some sort of naturalistic feeder or drainage device.
Which, in a sense, it quite possibly is.
For, at the other end of it, the retired Abbot,
If he is still alive, slowly continues to breathe.
Wishing to be no longer a burden to anyone,
Down there, quietly, he waits for enervation and death.
Indeed – perhaps they have even come to him already.

2

Going off to the hidden Temple to give thanks
For a recent, deserved promotion to high office,
He was so deep in prayer, perhaps, that he failed to notice
The killer who crept or leapt out from behind the broad tree
Which in a stately manner shaded some of the steps.
This rude churl knocked him down, hacked at his neck, and ran off
Bearing the august, shocked head, which was never recovered.
A veil lies over all its subsequent history.
Fortunately, after hours of careful investigation,
A unique strand of his hair was identified at the spot.
It was picked up and cherished; and, a little later,
Standing in for the head, it was buried with the body,
Helping thus to make good a crucial spiritual shortfall.


## Marine Impromptu

What was I doing at six o'clock last Wednesday?
Can I really not drum up a single detail?
I mean to say, we have only just now left
Friday morning behind, and I have lately come back
from a stroll through town, to buy some Danish pastries
then get some money from a bank which faces the sea.
To buy a newspaper too, of course. And the newspaper
tells me that at six o'clock last Wednesday evening
while a woman was crossing a road I know very well
(back in Glasgow) – a lorry struck and killed her.
My immediate thought was: oh, some poor old pensioner!
But no: she was younger than I am. My next thought was –
But I would rather repress what my next thought was.
Yes. I would rather repress what my next thought was.

A GOD'S BREAKFAST

## Count O'Donnell, I Presume?

Dear Count O'Donnell – or so one trusts you were;
for the fact is, I know nothing whatever about you –
except that such is the name which Robert Schumann
thought he recalled seeing ('if I'm not mistaken')
on the tombstone between the graves of Beethoven and Schubert –
and he claimed he almost envied you, who had somehow come to rest
between those vast making-unmaking neighbours, unknown –
long years before the site was changed to a children's playpark.

So there you are, roughly. Or were. One does one's best
to live decently, I suppose – or so one blankly assumes;
to bring in others with as few mistakes as possible,
make spaces for friends, do the job as well as you can;
and if people later visit your grave, or not,
or halt, or return, or pass it again, then so what?

## They All Turned Over in their Sleep

All right. So that beautiful house across the lane
is where the murders took place. On ordinary evenings,
sometimes the light was on, and sometimes it was off.

But look at the gorgeous attic on the villa next door to it!
I feel I would like to have occupied that attic.
Is one right to envy whoever did occupy that attic?

I dare say it depends on what one heard during the night.
One person? Two persons? Footsteps in the lane?

## The Failed Recluse

The child repeatedly jumping on the floor of the flat upstairs
might have wakened me up again this morning, I suppose;
had not, ten minutes before that, another, screaming child
been wrestled into a car parked exactly beside my window.

## La Belle Dame Sans Underpants

Midnight. More people laughing in the nearby corridor
of this foreign hotel. Here even the darkness
seems somehow different. Somehow so much livelier.
Off they go, overwhelmingly happy (by the sound of it)
with their own up-to-date example of modern life
in a complex minority language. Not to know it better
is the world's loss. Shall I drift back to sleep?
Should I put on the bedside lamp and try to read?
A dim, unnatural light seeps in through the thin curtain
and outlines various shapes – including the lamp,
with, leaning against its base, an oblong photograph.
Silence again. Only I in all this city
know what the picture is on that photograph –
as the noise of the same happy group now rings out in the street.


## 111

In a dream, I was talking to a black Norwegian athlete.
About Ibsen, alas. I kept trying to change the subject.
She grew shrill, and accused me of being patronising. But, really –
I just didn't want to tell her what I really thought about *Brand*.


## Yet Another Dazzling Non-Coincidence

The torch lies on the table beside the dresser.
The dresser on which stands a leather hippo, made in India.
The hippo which once made a young woman cry, 'Oh! A hippo!'
The torch which once made another woman cry, 'Oh! A torch!'

A GOD'S BREAKFAST

Look! Twenty years on, and that bus-stop where we met
is still there, in exactly the same spot on the pavement.
This time, two old women are waiting patiently beside it.

Hello: I am wearing shoes bought in Augsburg
and a shirt bought in Munich the year before that –
while I sit in a Glasgow bus in the very early morning
wondering why that man is lounging up there near a roof.

## Belmont Street

Slightly before we are quite sure that the builders
have indeed moved out, have indeed finished, the first signs
of human habitation are there – far more eagerly
even than the weeds sprouting up in abandoned corners.

Windows are suddenly lit. Plants have appeared in them.
Pictures are now to be seen in gaps between the curtains.
One accidentally catches a glimpse of something
moving; something no doubt eager and human.

Is there basic building work continuing here or not?
Is something more going to be done to those stairs and doorways?
Is the unnatural grass going to be clipped, for instance?
Oh! Look! Who can be opening that door?

## Christmas Day

I have phoned you up,
at different times,
from both those kiosks
at the far end of this street.

This evening, more cars
continue to sweep past them
to stop at the traffic-lights
just up ahead.

Or, if the lights
should happen to favour them,
they run straight through
without even stopping.

## From A to Z

Everything is more or less
a question of her.

Even that long low road
snaking away down there
beneath this sudden railway bridge –

indeed, did we not once
drive rather urgently along it
in her next-to-last car?

part of a hectic, late-night journey

but that's not quite what I meant.

Suddenly – yes, quite suddenly – almost a decade later,
I realise what it must have been I did wrong.
A different car hurries through a different street.
Within a couple of hours, I start to be fifty-one.


## Another Poem Found Scribbled in an Old Book

I have thought of you in towns where you have never been.
I have thought of you in rooms which you have never seen.
In one of which, sandwiched between two matching books,
There's a passionate letter which I have still not sent to you.


## The Tenth Symphony

1

We are sitting together in the growing dusk,
listening to loud music which does not quite exist.

2

Yes. It is a symphony composed after his death
by the Great Master. Not even extinction, it seems,
could quite manage to stop him from adding to our lives.

3

For a scholar has thoughtfully picked his way among
many pages of lines, suggestions and sketches;
and has slowly drawn out here into the half-light
something which perhaps the light itself half created.

4

Until, at last, there is a gap between the movements
and, still impassive, you shift slightly in your seat.

5

And suddenly I realise – yes, that silence is his!
That silence is certainly his, the great composer's!
That majestic silence, so full of unheard futures.